ROMANTIC REBEL

The Life and Times of George Sand

Romantic Rebel

THE LIFE AND TIMES OF

George Sand

BY FELIZIA SEYD

The Viking Press, New York

1940

TO

ARTHUR SEYD

CONTENTS

8 CONTENTS

Part Three: Compromise

ILLUSTRATIONS

PART ONE

The Dream That Was Individualism

PART ONE

The Dream That Was Individualism

*"Le plaisir que nous donne un artiste c'est
de nous faire connaître un univers de plus!"*

—MARCEL PROUST

CHAPTER ONE

The Ancestors

"Donc le sang des rois se trouve mêlé dans mes veines au sang des pauvres et des petits."

—GEORGE SAND: *Histoire de Ma Vie*

AMONG the cherished possessions of the Sand family to-day is a portrait of Maurice de Saxe, famous bastard of Augustus the Strong of Poland and the Countess Königsmarck, who by unorthodox but none the less real ties was the great-grandfather of George Sand. This is the story:

One of the last mistresses of the Maréchal Maurice de Saxe was a young actress, Mademoiselle de Verrières, who had given performances at his house as a member of a road company. Maurice took her away from the troupe, gave her a generous allowance, and set her up in style. When she bore him a daughter after a year—the grandmother of George Sand—he doubled her pension.

Victoire de Verrières was to become famous in the Paris *beau monde* in later years, but she had her origin in those

13

indefinable layers of society which the eighteenth century considered collectively as "the people." Her real name was Marie Rinteau and her early background remains a matter of conjecture. Women of her class were generally in a difficult position. Their means of livelihood were confined to peddling, sewing, embroidering, or laundry work. Their home life meant starvation, beatings, drunkenness, or prostitution. The one escape—the theater—presupposed a pretty face and a great deal of intelligence. Nor were its moral dangers less. The lucky girls who managed to become extras at the Comédie Française or the Opéra often made love a side line of their profession, for they could not exist on their salaries. On the other hand, if they were caught in a delicate situation, the police could not send them to the women's prison or shave their heads, for theatrical persons were safe from the authorities. Avenues were opened to them: there was a chance of finding a rich protector and of rising to more ostentatious heights until "their outer life no longer differed in glamour, luxury, and culture from that of the highest aristocracy." According to the brothers Goncourt they could even "become a power, counting their victims by the score, and showing themselves superior to the women in society in that they lent elegance to their debauchery, greatness to their vice, and managed their scandals with the grace and the courage of antique hetaerae." As a result society did not shrink from them, once they had "arrived." But what endurance, cleverness, and vitality were needed to make that dream come true! Mademoiselle de Verrières, who succeeded to a nice degree, deserves full respect.

She started her career with Maurice de Saxe, but the valiant Maréchal was not a faithful lover, nor was Victoire de Verrières very loyal to him. They eventually separated, the Maréchal, for valid enough reasons, even discontinuing his mistress's pension. However, Maurice's little daughter was less abruptly dismissed. She hardly ever saw her famous father again but was allowed, by parliamentary decree, to carry his name and call herself Marie-Aurore de Saxe. She grew up to be an attractive young woman and, with the Dauphine de France as protectress, was married at eighteen to the Count de Horn—a bastard of Louis XV.

George Sand has told us the story of this first marriage of her grandmother's. The experience was not a happy one. Fortunately for the bride, the young husband fell in a duel three weeks after the wedding and Marie-Aurore returned to live once more at her mother's. She had none of Mademoiselle de Verrières's dissolute inclinations and found it hard to adapt herself at home. Nevertheless she stayed until her mother died and then withdrew to a convent. Her inheritance was more than slight, consisting, according to George Sand, of a painted portrait of the Countess Königsmarck, the seal and snuff-box of the Maréchal de Saxe, and many unpublished verses by Victoire de Verrières's former paramours.

Marie-Aurore, beautiful and chaste, was also practical. At the age of thirty she married a second time: Monsieur Dupin de Francueil, an amiable widower of sixty-two who had been her aunt Geneviève's lover and had gained historic renown through his relationship with Madame d'Epinay, the benefactress of Rousseau. Marie-Aurore probably considered an elderly husband a guarantee for protection and peace. The future father of George Sand was then born, a beautiful son named after the Maréchal, and the mother might have lived happily if her husband had not inconsiderately died very soon.

This happened shortly before the Revolution. Marie-

Aurore again was a widow and again poor, for Monsieur Dupin, in the gentlemanly fashion of the times, had managed to squander most of his fortune, leaving just enough to buy a small estate in a rather secluded part of the province of Berry. The château of Nohant, near La Châtre, was purchased in the second year of the French Revolution for three hundred thousand inflated francs, and set up as a comfortable though not elaborate family homestead.

Besides herself and her son, Madame Dupin's household comprised at this time two other important members: Deschartres, tutor, philosopher, and general manager; and Julie the young chambermaid, whom George Sand was to remember as the type of all ambitious, inhibited, aging maids, living partly as a reflection of the praise and scoldings of her mistress, and partly as a reflection of the outer world as seen in the gossip and petty sensationalism of an improper literature. "Whenever I write my books," said George Sand, "I imagine some Julie will read them; all novels are ultimately written for chambermaids."

Under the care and supervision of this not-too-brilliant triumvirate, the young grandson of the Maréchal de Saxe grew up. He played the violin and danced well; he could also act. Madame Dupin had high hopes as to his future in society; he would bring the family back to fortune and fame. She sent him to Paris armed with introductions to influential friends, to his rich cousins on Monsieur Dupin's side, the Villeneuves, who received him with condescension. After a while he tired of waiting in the antechambers of society. Remembering that his ancestors were warriors and men of action, he thought of joining the army—the republican army, of course—which just then promised fair adventure under the leadership of General Bonaparte. He bought himself a green dolman and fine boots and enlisted as a private. His mother began to receive letters:

"I am no longer only the grandson of the Maréchal de Saxe but a soldier in the service of the Republic, and whatever interest is shown in me here I try to deserve well. As far as your position goes, my dear Mother, please don't go on considering yourself a suspected member of the old regime but the mother of a defender of the nation. You must begin to see things from this angle. . . . The army has not made a Jacobin of me but it has taught me that one must live without looking backward . . . that the loss of title and fortune is a small thing, and that it is a privilege to win through personal effort what was formerly a matter of birth."

The boy, who had been fourteen when the Terror was in full swing, had thus grown into a man who identified himself with the Revolution. Perhaps he had tired of the threadbare pretensions of being the grandson of the Maréchal de Saxe. This was only the beginning, however; there was worse in store for Madame Dupin. After a year of uneventful service in Belgian and Rhenish garrisons, Maurice crossed the Saint-Bernard with Bonaparte and the army and was made lieutenant the day of the battle of Marengo. Madame Dupin for once seemed reconciled to her son's career. She spent part of her meager funds to help with his expensive equipment and moved heaven and earth to further his advancement. For a while she heard laudable reports about him; then his superiors grew indifferent, showing a lack of interest that amounted to ostracism. When Madame Dupin discovered the basis for the intrigue it was too late to do anything about it. Maurice was then irrevocably caught in a misalliance.

He had met Sophie Delaborde in Milan, where she was the mistress of a French general. The young people fell in love; Sophie, another Manon, undid the fetters of her shame and from then on lived for love alone—that is, she followed Maurice from garrison to garrison, fighting poverty and intrigue, making a living by selling hats. Sophie did not mind the hardships; her father had run a poolroom and her grandmother was a certain Mother Cloquart who sold vegetables in the market. An orphan at fourteen, Sophie had followed the lines of Mademoiselle de Verrières's career but with less fortunate results. When she met Maurice she already had one illegitimate child. She bore him children too, but they did not live. Finally, when she was again faced with pregnancy, Maurice decided to marry her so that the child would stand a better chance. They were married a month before their daughter was born. The girl was called Aurore after the grandmother who ignored her. Nevertheless, said Sophie Delaborde: "The name will bring her luck." She was mistaken, for the name went down to limbo when Aurore at the age of twenty-eight adopted for herself and her children the sterner and more modern pseudonym of George Sand.

Not that this meant denial of background. In her autobiography George Sand set up a memorial to her ancestors, thankful, as she wrote about them, for the gifts of resistance and independence they left in her blood.

CHAPTER TWO

Childhood

MUSSET called the children born under the First Empire a nervous, pale, and passionate generation, conceived between two battles, and sent to school while drums rolled in the streets. "Occasionally their fathers would appear, press them against their gold-braided uniforms, put them down quickly, and be off to war again."

Aurore, born in 1804, was a true child of this epoch. The shadows of the imperial eagles fell across her crib, and her baby sleep was often disturbed by the bugle call of departing regiments. Her father would appear between campaigns glittering with decorations and immediately be off again. But the rest of her existence was unheroic enough. While the *pot-au-feu* simmered on the stove, filling the tiny Parisian apartment with its smell of onions and boiled cabbage, she busied herself picking straw out of the seat of an old chair and invented interminable stories of noble knights, beautiful ladies, magicians, and fairies, which she recited in a monotone.

Bolitho has written an excellent comment on the early background of Lola Montez which applies equally well to that of George Sand: "She was born (in 1818) in that ambiguous level of society, where, to survive, the first need is a concentrated imagination and a firm uncritical talent. Her father was an officer in a line-regiment, and further a ranker-lieutenant. That is, an aristocrat by courtesy, which was seldom shown him, without birth or fortune; required to live and think like a squire turned knight-errant in the space comprised by the married quarters and parade ground of a mean garrison town, on the pay and more than the limitations of a curate. Like his shirt under his uniform, his life, inside the official poetry of his situation, was thread-bare and embarrassed; his daughter was brought up with the curious mental adjustments produced by the situation. In spite of the contradiction that he had a fine uniform and was not quite a gentleman, such a life was a form of shabby-gentility, which is one of the usual recruiting grounds of adventurers as well as of poets, actresses, clerks, and congenital suicides."

The "shabby-gentility" seemed good enough for Sophie Dupin, who after four years of scrubbing, sewing, and miserly economies at home decided to join her husband Maurice on his next military campaign. She wanted to enjoy life, "be somebody," and not stay in an obscure corner while her husband roamed the world possibly to fall prey to some fine lady in a foreign garrison.

Maurice Dupin, hardened soldier of many fronts, warned her of war's hardships and danger, but Sophie's stubborn mind was set. Caroline, her first-born, illicit child, would be boarded out, while Aurore would travel with her parents.

Maurice, aide-de-camp to Murat, was just then ordered to Madrid. His wife and the four-year-old Aurore followed in the wake of the army. Adventure soon pressed in on them: robbers and bears threatened in the Pyrenees; near the Spanish border the night sky was red from the flames of burning villages; food was scarce and the travelers were reduced to eating raw onions. Once, while they stopped at an inn for fresh horses, they had a glimpse of Spanish royalty fleeing towards France.

But when Madrid was reached and the Dupin family installed in an upper-story apartment of a royal palace, the world of Aurore's fairy tales came true. The immense rooms had walls covered with red silk, the furniture was golden, and the huge crystal mirrors reflected the interior a hundredfold. Aurore's toys were bizarre, hand-painted dolls left behind by the royal children. Sophie, to please Murat, sewed a uniform for her daughter, who paraded before him in green dolman, white trousers, and red boots.

Sophie was pregnant again, and a few weeks later bore a brother for Aurore. The baby was born blind, and in her rage the mother held the Spanish doctor responsible. According to her he had crushed the child's eyes with his thumb. But there was no time to court-martial anyone. The country was rising in revolt against the foreign invaders; the Dupin family, along with the whole of Murat's army, was soon in wild retreat back across the Pyrenees. Heat, fever, thirst, and the rumbling of distant cannon filled the days and nights of that disastrous journey. The Dupins finally reached the Bay of Biscay and from there sailed by boat to the mouth of the Gironde. Early in August they arrived in Nohant. Madame Dupin *mère* was on the doorsteps to greet them.

The former Marie-Aurore de Saxe was still an impressive woman. Brilliantly powdered and rouged, she wore a blond wig which curled over her forehead. Her carriage

was erect and full of dignity, her conversation vivacious
and witty. But for her old-fashioned brown silk gown with
flat sleeves and a low waistline, no one would have thought
of her as a woman of the former regime.

The refugees, who arrived sick with the scabies and half
starved, were installed and quickly put at ease. A small side-
wing of the house was assigned to Maurice and his wife,
while Aurore slept in her grandmother's luxurious Louis
XV bed. Soon the child was well enough to play in the
garden, where she met her half-brother Hippolyte, a rough,
nine-year-old boy—illegitimate offspring of Maurice and a
scullery maid—who had been adopted into the Dupin
family.

There was a moment's breath for them, then the all-too-
delicate balance of the family's happiness and peace was
irrevocably destroyed. One evening while riding home from
La Châtre, Maurice was thrown from his horse and instantly killed. And only the week before, he and Sophie
had buried their blind infant son in the park under a linden
tree.

The first shock of horror and despair drove the two
Dupin women into each other's arms, yet the differences in
their character and upbringing did not allow for enduring
harmony. The grandmother, according to Aurore's description, was the typical eighteenth-century aristocrat, blond,
fair, very Germanic. She was the self-controlled, philo-
sophical, clever woman of the world who considered any
display of emotion a sign of bad breeding. Disciplined and,
if necessary, heroic, she represented the true classic type.
Aurore's mother was, in her daughter's words, "the tradi-
tionless child of the people, dark, ardent, petite, alert,
uneducated and uncontrolled, a bundle of emotions and prej-

udices, averse to any mental effort, without much consideration for others, yet eternally insisting on what was due
her." But she was also witty, warm, generous, capable with
her hands, and, given an occasion, enthusiastic without
limit. The daughter later developed many of her mother's
traits.

After a while the older woman suggested that her daugh-
ter-in-law return to Paris to take care of her child Caroline,
while Aurore remained in Nohant as her grandmother's
legal ward.

Little Aurore, frightened by the possibility of losing her
mother, slipped into Sophie's bedroom at night and begged
her with tears not to sell her to the strict old lady. Sophie,
pressed by circumstances, could only tell her that it was all
for the best, that life in Nohant would mean a good education and social advantages, while the future in Paris with
her mother and half-sister meant poverty and social dis-
grace. After a heartbreaking farewell the mother set out
alone for the north.

Aurore, left to the care of her grandmother and her father's childhood tutor Deschartres, felt bewildered and uncomfortable. She was told to hold herself straight, speak in
subdued tones, avoid the country dialect, wear gloves in
the garden, and address her elders with the formal *"vous."*
Much time had to be spent in her grandmother's boudoir,
where she must quietly sit at the old lady's feet. The room
was dark and stuffy, the curtains drawn against draft and
light, and the air heavy with benzoin fumes. The child
was soon plagued with headaches that drove her to hys-
terics.

Fortunately, some time each year was spent in Paris,
where Madame Dupin *mère* had a comfortable apartment.

The walls here were covered with blue brocades; rugs and curtains were of exquisite softness, and each room had its friendly fireplace.

But Grandmother's friends, belonging to the aristocratic and royalist Faubourg Saint-Germain, were less attractive. Sophie had called them derisively *"ces vieilles comtesses"*; to Aurore they seemed like her bizarre Spanish dolls with their pointed shoes, their old-fashioned clothes, their untidy wigs and bare arms. Dusty and old, with warts and wrinkles, they possessed either "an ardent leanness or a melancholy embonpoint."

Sunday evenings were spent at Uncle Beaumont's house. The Abbé de Beaumont, a half-brother of Marie-Aurore de Saxe, was a bastard of Mademoiselle de Verrières and the Maréchal de Turenne. His allowance secured him a comfortable existence in post-revolutionary Paris. His passion was food.

"The test of a good cook is an omelet," he used to tell his guests. "Remember Louis XV's pancakes? Richelieu said they were usually badly burnt, because the king did not know how to do them. It is because cooking demands a quality that kings do not possess—patience! By the way, my dear Victoire"—he would suddenly turn to his good-looking housekeeper—"don't you think our omelet contains a trifle too much nutmeg today?"

And Victoire would smile acquiescently while one of the elderly friends, Madame de Pardaillan, picking up the thread of the conversation, would wail: "Patience, Monseigneur! Who has patience nowadays? None of these modern barbarians knows anything about food anyway. When I remember what my mother used to tell us about the dinners of Madame de Pompadour!"

"Oh, Madame la Marquise de Pompadour ought to have

GEORGE SAND AS A CHILD
(Musée Carnavalet)

known about food," Uncle Beaumont would chuckle maliciously; "she was a butcher's daughter. . . . These carrots are excellent, Victoire; just the right size too, the size of a child's small finger."

Aurore, meanwhile, had slipped from the table and gone exploring in the big salon, which for reasons of economy was never opened. A lighted candle in her hand, she examined every corner of it: the dark draperies, the heavy furniture inlaid with mother of pearl and tortoise shell, the oil paintings—huge portraits by Largillière, Dutch still-lifes, and Italian landscapes.

When she emerged from her treasure-hunt the old people had settled down to their game of whist; the conversation had turned to cards, family connections, and—the Emperor.

The latter was an ever-ready target for their hatred and scorn. "Did you hear what Talleyrand said about him?"—"No, but the Empress's chambermaid told my niece this morning that Bonaparte slapped his wife in a fit of drunkenness!"—"The beast—he does not even respect the Pope; he is said to have boxed his ears."—"Well, in the words of Monseigneur Talleyrand, the beginning of the end is come."

The ten-year-old Aurore, who had been told to amuse herself with her uncle's snuff-box collection, resented this talk. The Emperor to abdicate? A new king to come, a Bourbon? Obscurely she sensed that such words betrayed the ideals her father had held; that his glory was linked with the glory of the Emperor, with the France of the Revolution.

"They are evil here," she thought. "Grandmother too. I love only my mother." And while her sleepy eyes were fixed on the miniatures of nymphs and shepherdesses, she

dreamed of tomorrow's visit with her mother—their walk
along the boulevards where there would be fresh air, gay
crowds, a puppet show, and trained dogs that danced on
their hind legs.

Under the Restoration, Grandmother's trips to Paris
came to an end. Her health began to fail and there were
symptoms of her money's failing too. She lived in her bedroom now, attended by two maids. Aurore was admitted for
a short visit at night when Madame Dupin was ready for
bed, adorned in lace cap, lace wrapper, and the jewelry of
the occasion. All day long Aurore was thrown upon her own
resources. Hippolyte had entered military service, and Deschartres, the pedagogue, was much too occupied with the
household accounts to bother about her education. But the
child found instruction elsewhere—and George Sand's
writings benefited by it.

The province of Berry with its hills and dales, twisted little brooks, and legend-haunted woods, was a lost section in
the center of France. It had kept much of its traditional
custom, dress, speech, and song. There was druid magic still
in the quiet woods, and the memory of the Gallic peasant
who had once plowed these fields was now alive in the bar-
baric rhythm with which the Berry peasant drove his oxen.
These people wore clothes spun from flax grown on their
own acres; they had second sight, believed in ghosts and
"the Evil One" who roamed the highways at night; their
dialect went back to the French of Rabelais.

At night the villagers gathered in the community barn,
watching the old flax-comber work and listening to his stories. More often than not, Aurore was present, spellbound
by the tales. There was always an added climax when someone in the audience got up and verified a point. "Yes, I have

seen the Evil One myself, at the second turn of the
Châtre road!" or: "A will-o'-the-wisp led old André astray
and he drowned in the swamp," or: "Last night enchanted
rats piled up the priest's beans into mysterious heaps and no
one knows why." The mystic and imaginative soul of the
Berry peasant, in many ways still purely Celtic, yielded an
inexhaustible fund of stories that were avidly absorbed by
the child's mind.

In Aurore's life, dream and reality began to merge into
one. She had always been able to escape into a dream-state at
will. Staring at the fire-screen in her grandmother's sitting-
room, she was able to find whole landscapes . . . "woods,
meadows, rivers, cities of gigantic size and bizarre architec-
ture, and gardens with profusions of flowers, but mostly
green, black, and blue roses." Now, in ranging over the
whole countryside, her imagination seized at random on
anything—Plaisir the swineherd, for instance. Was he a
human or a gnome? Hidden behind the hedge, Aurore
crouched for hours, watching as he stood motionless in the
fields, the trident, the sign of his profession, in his hand,
while the darlings of Circe grunted softly at his feet. He
was a great magician, charming his beasts with his song
—a savage melody with the power and weirdness of a druid
incantation.

In times of supervision, when she was kept at home for
longer hours, and had to submit to the severe discipline,
even beatings, of the ill-humored chambermaid Julie, there
would be violent outbursts of temper. One day she declared: "I have had enough of Nohant . . . I want to go to
Paris and join my mother." As a punishment she was confined to her room for a week; then her grandmother sum-
moned her and told the child what she thought of her
mother.

"She began to tell me of her own and her son's life, then described my mother's life as she saw and understood it. She had no pity and understanding; yet poor people know temptations, errors, and accidents which are incomprehensible to a rich person. Grandmother did not refer only to her past but intimated awful mysteries in Mother's present life. In the end, exhausted, choked with tears, she said that my mother was a lost person and that I too was headed for the abyss."

Aurore, stunned, bathed in sweat, and unable to speak, was seized with convulsions. Yet when she had calmed down again, she hated and reproached only herself. A week later her grandmother took her to Paris, allowed her to see her mother once more, and then put her to school at the convent of the English Sisters.

Aurore remained within its walls three years, never asking permission to visit anyone outside. Her grandmother had forbidden her to see her mother. Aurore therefore would visit no one at all. Spite, obstinacy, pride, and independence were like so many dragon's teeth sown within her.

CHAPTER THREE

Birth of a Soul

AFTER her three cloistered years Aurore returned to Nohant, a young woman, accomplished, well bred, and eager for the intellectual companionship of her clever and cultivated grandmother. But Madame Dupin, now so clearly necessary as mental and spiritual guide to her granddaughter, was no longer able to fill that place. A stroke had paralyzed her body. On coming home, Aurore found herself reduced to the companionship of Deschartres and Julie the maid. Aside from the daily care of her grandmother, she had nothing but "the practice of religion and the study of philosophy."

Madame Dupin, in accordance with her own classical upbringing, had taught her granddaughter to study methodically, to summarize her reading, and to make marginal criticisms. And in the manner once approved by the pedantic Maréchal de Saxe, Aurore applied herself to the study of her grandmother's library books—to the works of Aristotle, Dante, Bacon, Shakespeare, Locke, Leibniz, and Rousseau. The convent-bred girl did so with qualms. Her recent education had made her an ardent follower of the Abbé Gerson, whose ascetic doctrines acclaimed mental self-abasement and decried intellectual vanity. But one day, while reading Chateaubriand, Aurore was moved by a broader concept of Christianity, one that glorified the mind. "Elevate your soul, develop your faculties, devote yourself to mankind, life! Science, art, and beauty are all manifestations of God. It is necessary to understand God in order to love Him!" These were the precepts of quasi-heretics, of men like Spinoza, who had the audacity to apply reason rather than faith to their concept of God.

With Deschartres's help Aurore began the study of Leibniz, but, knowing that her previous education had been inadequate training for this philosopher, she also took up mathematics, physics, and chemistry. She learned a little natural history, too, and collected butterflies and pebbles. All told, she seemed on the verge of becoming one of those "charming little monsters" who, like Madame de Genlis, could do simply everything: embroider a canvas, play the harp, practice blood-letting, discourse on geology, and write verses. But Aurore soon tired of the dry demands of pure philosophy; the monads of Leibniz whirled unrecognized through her brain, butterflies and pebbles accumulated dust in the drawer, and the little cricket caged in her room languished. The imagery of poets like Dante and Byron proved a pleasant relaxation while the communist Mably was disregarded for the time being; Franklin won her enthusiastic regard; Voltaire was forbidden (she had promised her grandmother not to read him until she was thirty); the great revelation was Rousseau.

Rousseau has been called the true father of Romanticism; more precisely put, he was a strong opponent of the extreme

rationalism of the eighteenth century. "The senses are de-
ceptive, the rational mind alone is able to perceive truth";
so Descartes and all his followers had taught. Voltaire and
the Encyclopedists, Locke and the practical-minded English
empiricists, had put their faith in experimental science,
made fun of metaphysical speculation, and subjected the
least emotion to critical analysis. Truth for them was in
physics and mathematics; their religion was "natural philosophy"; morality became a matter of calculation; "spiritual" motives were denied.

Against these discouraging concepts Rousseau set his
theory of the innate goodness of man, a goodness that lay
beyond his reasoning powers. He believed that man was
more than a mechanical apparatus, that he could reach the
perfection that lay within him by developing all his faculties. No real development could, however, be accomplished
under the present form of society, for bourgeois society
based on greed stifled man's original goodness and fathered
only his evil passions. In fact man's whole historic and cultural background was rotten and had to be abandoned. Only
a new democratic society, based on political equality and an
education with its precepts rooted in pity and altruism,
could guarantee the new and wholly liberated individual.
Back to nature! Or, rather, back to human kindness, which
is man's original and true form of being.

Aurore's adolescent soul, which yearned for a world built
on emotion rather than on reason, found in Rousseau's philosophy all the answers to its demands. Her heart was ready
to embrace all mankind and do away with inequality and
social injustice in the world. Besides, Rousseau's philosophy
offered a solution for her own problems in mental and social
adjustment by breaking up the confining universe that the
Church and her home influences had built up in her. Rous-

seau gave the lie to her grandmother's social prejudices and conventions. As far as the Church was concerned, "its spirit was no longer in me. Perhaps it had never really existed there."

As a disciple of Rousseau, Aurore had become a liberal, and liberalism and Catholicism were just then badly at odds. Greece and Italy, fighting for their national freedom, found the Pope in alliance with their chief enemies—the imperial House of Habsburg and the Turkish Sultan. The Pope in alliance with despotism? Was this compatible with the Christian dogma? Aurore's answer was an energetic No! Christianity must forever side with the rebels and the oppressed, for these hold a primary claim on progress and liberty!

Aurore's outer life was simple. She supervised the household and the farm property. She also had certain duties towards the cottagers and peasant tenants. When Deschartres, acting as a self-appointed doctor, went visiting in the village to set broken bones, bandage sores, and lend a hand in childbirth, Aurore was a capable and willing assistant. A friend of hers, a young medical student, had lent her a child's skeleton so that she might learn some elementary anatomy.

Her favorite sport was riding. She rode for hours on her stallion Pépé, wearing out the accompanying groom and the horses but never herself. In the autumn she and Deschartres went hunting. Long before sunrise, with pistol and net they would be patiently lying in hiding for quail.

The peasants near Nohant and the people of La Châtre thought her way of living odd and extravagant, and when she came to town she was watched and cackled over. "Here she comes, the crazy witch who goes hunting in men's clothes and with drawn pistols . . . shooting peasants and children so that she may drink their blood, digging up corpses at midnight, and riding up to the high altar on her devil's stallion. She is a demon who practices black magic; she never sleeps."

The "demon," however, had a dowry of half a million francs, and there were sons, badly pressed for money, who needed rich wives. The pious hens decided to be friendly after all and to return Aurore's nod when they met her in town. But there were crises. Public tension and disapproval came to a climax at a village dance where Aurore had too obviously championed a woman of bad reputation. The self-respecting peasants tried to snub Aurore, and a brawl would have resulted if friends had not spirited her away.

Later at home she discussed the incident with Deschartres. When he suggested greater circumspection in the future, Aurore exclaimed furiously: "I do not care to be cautious! . . . Caution is a gift and a prerogative of certain tempera-ments. I want to be guided by my conscience rather than by prudence, especially in a situation like this when the public is too prejudiced to meet the case squarely. I am fully pre-pared for the consequences."

In order to simplify matters she reasoned that she had better live in noble seclusion and shun society altogether. To renounce her La Châtre friends meant no sacrifice to her; on the contrary, their dinner invitations bored her and she was glad to saddle her horse when midnight came and ride back through the night—alone.

In her autobiography George Sand has left a dramatic account of those lonely meditations on the Châtre road. All the demons of doubt and unbelief were unleashed under the pale summer moon. She would analyze what she had learned from Rousseau and Leibniz and at the same time ask God and the stars what trend things earthly and un-

earthly were taking. From Descartes to Rousseau the phi-
losophers had preached the infallibility of the individual
soul, but it was a melancholy and frightening knowledge.
Aurore, as she stood at the crossroads of La Châtre, raised
her arms in anguish and wondered whither her new wisdom and intellectual independence would lead her. Nor was
this plight hers alone at this time. All over the country
promising young men, the artists of the coming generation,
were asking similar questions. Perturbed and confused by
the birth-pangs of their Romantic souls, they were nevertheless preparing to emerge with more than the ordinary
portion of self-adulation.

Aurore knew all too well this sense of superiority, which
was one of the curses and blessings of her generation. She
loved to consider the difference between herself and her environment: how miserable, spiteful, and stupid most of her
contemporaries were, even those whose dinner table she had
just left. Their calculating and ungrateful minds knew no
pity or generosity. Not one among them would give to
Aurore the sympathy she herself would grant the most miserable of beggars—sympathy, "that heavenly dew which is
as necessary for the soul as food and air are for the body."
She needed affection, a companion spirit— "das auslösende
Gemüt"; she suffered from spiritual and physical loneliness.
But there was no one in La Châtre worthy of her. Or was
there? A new doubt assailed her. She might not be superior
after all. She might be as hollow-minded as the rest. She
might be worse, for she had her insensate vanity. True,
there were her mystical urges to defend her, her vague
idealism, her love of truth and freedom. But did they prove
that she belonged to the chosen, that she was more pious,
sensitive, intelligent than others? That her eagerness to

help was not part of her vanity and her kindness to others merely lack of discrimination?

If she could have a sign, if God would signal to her! She would gladly walk the thorns after the saints and prophets. But God hid His face from her, like the moon of her midnight rides hiding behind a curtain of clouds. "Nothing, not a face, not a voice, not a shadow was in this darkness where I wandered."

Her grandmother died at Christmas 1821 after having duly confessed and received extreme unction. Not that she counted on saving her soul and facilitating her entrance into eternity by this last religious gesture; she simply wanted to avoid all signs of singularity in these days when a Bourbon court in France made for Catholic and monarchic feeling. Whatever she was offered in her last moments by the Church she accepted in the skeptical spirit of a true Voltairian: "One meets these things with decency and respect, but does not believe in them!"

Perhaps she might have changed Aurore's life if she had lived longer. Her cool and rational character was in sharp contrast to that of her own nonconformist ancestors; she was chaste, but with the miserly chastity of those all-too-reasonable virgins who despite their well-stocked lamps have no worlds to illuminate. Her ambitions ran along sterile lines of social power and success, were ultimately responsible for ruining her son's career, and would have hampered the granddaughter, who was charged for an early rebellion not only against social conventions but against society itself.

If we may compare Marie-Aurore de Saxe with any of her ancestors, it is with that haughty and ambitious grandmother of hers—the famous Aurore de Königsmarck whose heart did not break when Augustus the Strong failed her but who emptied her purse in furthering the mad schemes of her son Maurice of Saxony in Kurland and Russia. There is much in Madame Dupin *mère* to remind us of the adventurous Swedish countess who was above all an ambitious woman, but who died a cool and skeptical death as Abbess of Quedlinburg and was buried in her last court dress of red brocade.

Owing to an insufficiently precise stipulation in her grandmother's last will, Aurore was returned to the guardianship of Sophie Dupin. But life in Paris with this mother, formerly so eagerly sought, proved very difficult. Sophie had little understanding of her daughter's culture and character. She drove Aurore's maid and her pet dog from the house, took away her books, and tyrannized over her without rhyme or reason. Periods of tenderness and confidential outbursts alternated with scenes of unexplained wrath and jealousy. Sophie had grown into an elderly matron whose harassing restlessness communicated itself to everything and everybody around her. Each day found her with a new dress, scarf, hairdress, or even hair color. A hat or dress bought in the morning would be cut up and altered in the evening, to be changed again an hour later. Everything grew dull and tasteless in a little while, even her role as a mother.

She had made the acquaintance of the Duplessis, a well-to-do cultivated family in Melun who owned a house and a factory. After one or two visits with these kind and well-meaning people Sophie decided to leave Aurore with them for good, saying that she could no longer bear to see her sad face at home. Madame Duplessis took pity on the girl, who might one day be richly endowed but in the meantime had not one decent dress to wear. She replenished Aurore's wardrobe from her own and allowed the girl to buy the books she craved.

The Duplessis had a large circle of friends, and there for the first time Aurore enjoyed society. Several young men courted her unobtrusively. Among them was Casimir Dudevant, in Aurore's words "a slender, quite elegant officer, gay in character and military as to bearing." The Duplessis considered him agreeable and afforded Aurore and him every opportunity to know one another.

Casimir was not a bad match. Natural son of the Baron Dudevant of Guillery in Gascony, he had been adopted by his father and made his heir; at least he could look forward to a small inheritance. He and Aurore became good friends although neither love nor passion entered into their affection. But those emotions might only prove embarrassing in a marriage of convenience. The acquiescence of the Duplessis encouraged the betrothal. Aurore also realized that marriage would mean escape from her mother's tyranny.

When all had been decided Sophie Dupin was called in to give the blessing that was legally necessary. She objected, of course, enlarging any obstacle she could think of, insisting that Casimir had been a waiter and was no suitable match for an heiress to half a million francs. In the end she tired of her opposition as she had tired of every other consistent effort, and the marriage took place in September 1822. Accompanied by Aurore's half-brother Hippolyte, the couple left for Nohant full of the best domestic intentions. Their model ménage was to emulate the married happiness of the Duplessis.

CHAPTER FOUR

Rebellion

"ONE cool rainy autumn day three silent persons sat dreaming around the fireplace inside a little castle of the *département* of Brie, seriously occupied with watching the burning wood in the grate and the slowly moving hands of the clock on the mantelpiece. Two of the guests seemed to yield without resistance to the heavy boredom of the place but the third showed signs of open rebellion: his movements were restive, he stifled a yawn, and with the fire-tongs thrust at the crackling log as if thrusting out at the general enemy."

This is the beginning of Aurore's first novel, *Indiana*, written at Nohant during six rainy weeks of the fall of 1831. The book is filled with the gloom and depression of a bored country household, and the main characters show a curious resemblance to Monsieur and Madame Dudevant.

Casimir is represented by Delmar, "an elderly discharged colonel, spirited and still good-looking though heavy and bald and with the terrifying expression of a man and mas-

ter before whom everybody trembles—wife, dogs, and servants"; and Aurore is Indiana, Delmar's nineteen-year-old
wife, "transparent, pale, sad, and very young-looking beside her elderly husband—a flower blooming in an antique
vase!" Indiana's life with Delmar is frustration and rebellion, as was Aurore's life with Casimir. The novel, written
after nine years of married life, gives us a pretty accurate
picture of what the Dudevants' home life had been from
the very start.

Whose fault was it that their plans of happiness were
never realized? They had started their new life full of good
intentions. Casimir was economical, orderly, systematic, like
an old soldier. He kept the place in order, had the walls pa-
pered and the furniture freshly upholstered. He straight-
ened out the crooked garden paths and shot the decrepit dogs
and shabby peacocks which dirtied the lawn and the best
rugs in the drawing-room. He was kind and gay as long as
everybody bent under his will; crude and brutal as soon as
he drank. Horses and hunting were his main interests,
and Aurore's intellectual inclinations irritated and bored
him. Some nights his orgies, in which he was willingly assisted by Hippolyte, made the house tremble. Occasionally
there was a spree with one of the female servants. More
dangerous still—he was inclined to speculate with Aurore's
money.

Aurore was not a clinging wife. She had not been in love
when she married him and the lack of real affection soon
made itself felt. She raised numerous objections and demands which were incomprehensible to Casimir, but stub-
bornly insisted upon by his wife. She would not yield the
reins of the household to him, she would not renounce all
claims to her legal possessions. She had queer ways of behavior, calling for such comments as: "Don't be singular!

. . . Don't be extravagant. . . . Why do you want Holy Thursday on Easter Sunday?"

At first they did not realize how ill-mated they were. Life only seemed very boring when they were together. They remedied this by visiting a good deal at the homes of the Duplessis in Melun or the elder Dudevants in Guillery. A winter spent in Paris cost them thirty thousand francs, admittedly paid out of Casimir's pocket. It was half of his marriage settlement from his family.

When their first child Maurice was born (June 30, 1823) they retired to Nohant again and for a while their happiness seemed more secure. The baby occupied Aurore's restless mind and made her forget the disillusions and disappointments of her young married life. But Maurice was soon weaned away from his mother's immediate care, stood on his own feet, and spoke his own language. Aurore, finding her days less occupied, looked around for new sources of interest and found there were none.

Some of her childhood friends from La Châtre—the amiable Duvernet, gigantic Fleury, Rollinat, Papet the nabob who owned a castle in the neighborhood, and the botanist Néraud, called Malgache, whose dahlias she had stolen as a child—these close friends were always ready to devote time to her. To divert her in time of moodiness and dissatisfaction, several of them stimulated her into making literary efforts—an autobiography and a novel, never published. But it was not enough to carry her out of the impasse of her married life.

A strange disease took hold of her; she had hemorrhages and believed herself tuberculous. To help restore her health the Dudevant family decided to spend the summer in the Pyrenean resort, Cauterets. Aurore left home with melancholy feelings: "Good-by, Nohant! I may never see you again."

Cauterets with its high mountain altitude not only gave her back her health but started her on her life of passion. Among the more distinguished guests of the little resort was Aurélien de Sèze, a young lawyer from Bordeaux, a man of excellent background and promising future, but otherwise of no outstanding importance. At least from the description left by Aurore we derive the impression of a well-bred, rather correct young man of the world who had none of the Romantic extravagances of Aurore's later loves.

Monsieur de Sèze, who was visiting his fiancée's family in Cauterets, found himself so completely transported by Aurore's questioning dark eyes that he forgot his duty. On the terrace of Saint-Savin, with its vista of the rich plain of Lourdes, he tenderly put his arm around her waist and dared to touch her lips with his. For a moment Aurore was uncertain as to what course to take, but then she remembered the good advice of the English nuns in Paris and their threats of eternal damnation. The seducer was sent on his way, or rather he was told that there could be no question of sin and adultery. Their affection must remain pure and spotless. Their souls alone must embrace, not their lips. Noble and resigned, their passion would stay outside the pale of human error and confusion—forever!

Aurore's great platonic love for Aurélien de Sèze lasted five years and helped her over many rough spots of her married life. The lovers wrote regularly and visited each other in Nohant and Bordeaux, but not one passionate gesture spoiled the purity of their relationship. Whatever passion there was found utterance in the written word only. Aurore's words, for that matter, are quite unrestrained: "I love you as I shall never love again!"

"Every fiber of my heart vibrates with yours, for you and I are one single being, one soul, one life, and if we were at the opposite poles of the earth, this divine sympathy would yet unite us again."

"My thoughts are fastened on you as if by magic, they follow you, surround you. You feel and breathe them, do you not? Ah, tell me that your life is as enchanted as mine, that no work is too dry, no duty too tiresome."

Casimir knew about Aurore's love, even saw her faint with emotion once or twice when Aurélien arrived on a visit. He treated the whole affair with surprising tact and good will and proved such an exemplary husband that Aurore had full confidence in him. When he left on a business trip during the first crucial months of Aurélien and Aurore's friendship, she wrote to him reassuringly: "Yes, because you are kind, generous, and decent you merit the same treatment in return. My arms are yearning for you . . . my heart is yours. . . . Are you satisfied with this? Come back soon. Don't worry, and have faith in me. Have confidence in the future. Sleep in peace. And promise me that from now on you will be happier with me."

Casimir showed himself docile and yielding enough at this time. There is talk of his shedding tears when Aurore discussed his shortcomings with him. He promised to do better and even submitted to the new terms which his wife communicated to him under points one, two, three, etc. Yes, he will listen when she plays the piano; he will study philosophy and languages and discuss books and theories with her. Aurore may continue to correspond with Aurélien, who for his part pledges eternal friendship to Casimir. After this Aurélien wrote less passionate letters but they contained many assurances of respect and affection for Casimir. He sent cough drops for the baby and knitting wool for

Aurore and in return begged for a pair of embroidered suspenders as his old ones were in a state of dilapidation.

We do not know what his feelings were when he came to Nohant in September 1828 and found that the Dudevants expected another child. He was present when the baby, Solange, was born. Perhaps Aurore asked him to stay, perhaps she needed somebody to confide in. Her marital relations had become more difficult than ever. Casimir the day after Solange was born was overheard arranging a rendezvous with the kitchen maid.

For two more years Aurélien remained the moral support of Aurore's life, "the third corner of my existence—God, he, and I!" Finally, in the year 1830, their great friendship came to a definite end because, as Aurore says, this superhuman striving for a divine love had tired her friend.

"When the calm but irrevocable separation between us had taken place I tried to continue my life, which after all had not changed outwardly. But it was impossible."

Now that her life was empty of love she realized the drawbacks of her marriage. Casimir through the years had grown more and more unbearable; his drunken orgies and love affairs were the talk of the countryside. One day Aurore chanced upon his will, which he must have concocted in a fit of utter wrath, and it was this revelation of Casimir's innermost thoughts that precipitated the break.

"My God, what a testament!" Aurore wrote. "His curses for me, and nothing else. All his ire, his brutality, his complaints about the perversions of my character were collected here. It was like a dream. I would never have thought myself so contemptible. But this general condemnation roused me out of my lethargy and I told myself: to live with a man who neither respects nor trusts me is as useless as trying to bring a corpse back to life."

She decided that Boucoiran, her children's tutor, should stay with the children in Nohant and supervise their education and their health. "If Solange has an attack of the croup at night, give her milk of almonds. . . .

"Of course I don't expect to leave my children for long. It is only a momentary stratagem. Nor do I expect to close up the house in Nohant. The coachman and the butler with their wives may remain. . . . Two horses, two cows, etc., are sufficient for their needs. Six months a year I shall spend with my husband and my children at Nohant; Casimir perhaps will become a little more circumspect as a result of my course of action. He has behaved as if he could not bear me. Now that I know he actually can't, I want to leave. Naturally he is upset, but so much the worse for him."

The yearly allowance needed by Aurore for her Paris stay was three thousand francs. The sum was small but the Dudevant budget could not encompass more. Aurore also hoped to find some possibilities of earning money in Paris. If her needlework and drawings would not sell she might try her hand at writing. She had already made a first attempt at writing.

"I hope to create for myself a literary career," she told her friends when they questioned her on her Paris plans. She left Nohant on January 4, 1831, expecting to be absent for three months. She stayed away longer.

CHAPTER FIVE

Carnaval Macabre

THE January night she spent in the coach that took her north seemed interminable to Aurore. A cheerless moon stood over the frozen swamps and the stage jerked in the snow-covered tracks. The trees cast wavering shadows on the road and occasionally a rabbit jumped away from the high lumbering wheels, seeking shelter in the dark fields. With only a silent priest and a sleepy young girl as traveling-companions Aurore had ample time to ruminate on the events of the last days: the quarrels with Casimir, the preparations for her trip, and the tearful parting with her children. The last especially was the bitter price she had had to pay for her new freedom, and that freedom for the moment seemed transitory and questionable. Besides—it was desperately cold in the stage-coach.

Drawing her cover tighter around her knees, she gazed into the frozen night. Ghosts seemed to be abroad in these dark hours. She remembered the story her grandmother used to tell about the early road conditions in the Orléans

region. The corpses of thieves and robbers, including those
of women bandits, dangled from gallows set up by the road-
side, their hair and rags swinging in the breeze. The roads
were safe enough now, but was life—the life that awaited
her in Paris? The future seemed dark and threatening at
this moment, and a yearning for protection, for the security
and peace of her childhood, made her weep. But her tears
flowed gently and so silently that neither of her two companions was aware of them.

The Paris of 1830 has been painted as a Romantic carnival where ideas and champagne flowed with equal abundance, where each day saw the birth of a new philosophy
and a new political system, where painters, poets, reformers,
and rebels were constantly producing something extraordinary.

There was restlessness indeed under the newly established regime of Louis-Philippe. Owing to the government's
vaguely outlined policies, the political parties had embarked
on a ruthless struggle for supremacy. And the revolutionary
spirit, set free under a temporary anarchy, made for a rich
crop of political and aesthetic manifestations which seemed
at the time very promising. But the carnival of "ideas" and
fashions was less amusing and less brilliant than some senti-
mentally reminiscent poets in later years would have us believe. It was deeply tinged with the yellow of biliousness
(the *couleur à la mode* adopted by the young Romantics as
a sign of spiritual fitness) and it was to end with dreadful
irony in a dance of death—the cholera plague of 1832.

After the abdication of Charles X, who was altogether
too reactionary even for the reactionary middle class, Louis-
Philippe had become ruler of France less by his own exer-
tions than by the clever machinations of Thiers, who told

him that to become King of France was the best he could do
for the moment. Louis-Philippe of Orléans was a simple little man, rather fat, with a head like a pear. With his large
umbrella tucked under his arm he used to walk the Paris
streets and in true patriarchal manner shake hands and converse with those who greeted him. His years of exile, when
he had been a teacher of languages, had not embittered him
but left him with a professorial air. According to the ideas
of the liberal party that forced him to the throne, he was a
most fitting head for a country with democratic aspirations.
He would begin by restoring the liberal constitution of the
country and then he would lead them all to brotherhood and
prosperity.

He had a wonderful beginning. Lafayette, a tricolor in
his hand, embraced him in view of the populace of Paris
and cried: "The Charter will now come true!" Lafayette
also immediately reorganized the National Guard so that
the new regime would have a military body on which to rely
in times of need; the National Guard had always been the
backbone of republicanism, and Lafayette had taken particular pride in this. All Frenchmen between twenty and
sixty were ordered to join the militia, that is, all Frenchmen who could pay for their own uniforms. This, of course,
excluded the working-classes, which was not Lafayette's
intention; but the king thus found an unobtrusive means of
keeping the National Guard a middle-class institution. "We
desire to keep a just middle road," he said calmly.

The middle class had after all made him; he gave the
middle class its due. In its interest he not only kept Lafayette from radicalizing the National Guard; he also opposed universal suffrage. The franchise was extended to in-
clude those with incomes of two hundred francs, but no less,
thus giving the smallest property-owner a chance to have a

say in the government, but leaving the working-class without the ballot. Chateaubriand predicted: "This will last fifteen years; our nephews will know the deluge!"

With the government thus vaguely defined as a government of the *juste-milieu*, the opposition parties of the right and left immediately began an open assault upon it, seeking to overturn the regime that was hardly born. Strikes, plots, and rebellions were the order of the day. Louis-Philippe, who in the meantime had given up his paternal conversations in the streets, installed as prime minister a liberal banker, Laffitte, who was expected to meet the country's democratic desires as well as the needs of business expansion. But the bourgeoisie considered the gesture a weak one, talked defeatism, and hid their jewels. Paris was more restless than ever. After the commemorative service for the Duc de Berry, in February 1831, at which the clergy of Paris had been too much in evidence, the populace stormed the churches and plundered even the archbishop's palace. The streets became unsafe. Gangs of hoodlums and vagabonds, with their strongholds on the outskirts of the city, joined the various demonstrations of unemployed and strikers and kept the riots and insurrections going for days. The peddlers of incendiary pamphlets, the famous *crieurs de journaux*, filled the streets with their inflammatory cries, while the great satirical newspapers, such as *Le Charivari*, *La Caricature*, and *Le Corsaire*, furthered the unrest with fanatical diatribes of their own. They did not shrink from inciting to murder, incendiarism, and overthrow of the king.

Laffitte, to master the growing chaos, turned for help to the Chamber, which in true democratic fashion was ever ready to suspect invasion of its own rights but did nothing to remedy an untenable situation. "They were an assembly of men honest but suspicious, attacking the government

without wanting to overthrow it—one day approving, the
next day blaming." The big financial interests soon felt the
whole social structure of the country to be endangered. Fear
as well as the competition of English mills had, for instance,
brought the wages in the Lyon silk industry down to a pit-
tance. The working-men went on strike. An army of sixty
thousand foot soldiers, sixty cannon, five thousand cavalry-
men was mobilized to meet them. The starved and desperate
working-men resisted and were shot down.

The country at large was thoroughly disturbed. The re-
volts were over, but business was still caught in a recession
movement. Laffitte had to yield his place to Casimir Périer.
Périer, a banker and a liberal under Charles X, proved to be
the new broom once he came into power. He used troops
and police, not the reluctant National Guard, to fight the
proletarian insurrections; he silenced the street-venders and
the cocky and critical cabarettists; he expelled the vagabonds, shipped the unemployed to their native districts, and
taught the police to use their clubs. Périer, a man of courage and temperament, endowed with unusual political vision, played the strong man, not to re-establish reaction but
to stabilize the Louis-Philippe democracy. Yet by destroying some of the abuses resulting from the anarchic confusion of the day he naturally seemed to assume the stature of
a high-handed dictator, especially in his dealings with the
Chamber of Deputies. Again there was no co-operation
from these quarters. Périer, the "perpetual professor of
energy," had to use all his spiritual force to overcome the
"cowardice and stupidity" of his co-workers. Trying to
rouse their opposition against the Republican party, the
Bonapartists, and other revolutionaries, he told the Chamber that "it is fear that serves the parties, aggrandizes, nay,
creates them, for it is fear that creates belief in their power."

When he had accomplished his task, that is, paralyzed most of the opposition (thus quelling a main source of unrest) and broached an energetic policy of economic expansion, the cholera killed him. Louis-Philippe, who was not displeased to be rid of his powerful prime minister, said without regret: "Périer dead? Is it good or bad luck? I do not know."

The Republicans knew it was luck for them.

The Republicans had been the left wing of the so-called *parti du mouvement*, opposing the government. It is here we come to the source from which the young Romantic liberals drank deeply. The Republican party program, even under Charles X during the 20's, demanded universal franchise, equal educational opportunities, the abolition or restriction of private property, social insurance, the right of free association, etc. Later they opposed the *laissez-faire* policies of the Louis-Philippe government, believed in state ownership, in the supervision and co-ordination of private enterprise, and also aimed from the beginning at the overthrow of that regime. They were helped by former members of Bonapartist and Jacobin societies, and they were even more eagerly aided by the growing artist generation which knew enough about Rousseau to insist that the dignity of humanity was dependent on its living in full individual liberty. Their slogans called for the defense of freedom endangered under Louis-Philippe's bourgeois society, proclaimed the struggle against king as well as bourgeois, and asserted that only a republican form of government would bring freedom and humane conditions.

Many of these youngsters had a background like that of Victor Hugo, who, with a Royalist mother, had at first been a Royalist and a Catholic, but then, after his Bonapartist father, turned insurgent with the popular tide. Their artistic vocabulary quickly adapted itself to the revolutionary vocabulary of the day. The franchise striven for in politics was likewise demanded in the arts. "Romanticism means liberalism in art!" said Hugo, who called the classics "the ultras." In the preface to his play *Cromwell* (1827) he had announced the new revolutionary program for poetry and the drama. Shakespeare was the ideal pattern (Hugo considered himself the Shakespeare of France at twenty-five). "What will the drama be like? First of all it will not be tragedy only, it will mingle tears and smiles." There need be no unity of place or time either, nor will the drama refrain from mixing the sublime with the ridiculous. "From the fecund alliance between the beautiful and the ugly, the tragic and the comic, will the drama be born." Nor should rhyme be shackled any longer by an artificial metrical foot. All laws in art must be reconsidered. Art is free and all-powerful as nature itself. "All that is in nature is in art too. Nature and truth are one! But truth is not absolute reality; you must be selective in joining the beautiful to the characteristic, the characteristic being the most distinctive and essential trait of an object."

Like the trumpets before Jericho, Hugo's declarations actually destroyed the walls of classicist rules. They set a new literary era in motion, which ultimately led to dadaism, but at least it let the poet breathe as freely as he wanted to. "The rose is as true as the cabbage!" he could declare triumphantly, and nobody thereafter could contradict him.

The young playwrights who tried to follow the new Romantic recipes of Hugo did their best to live up to the standards set by their great forerunner, Shakespeare—but they did not produce Shakespearean dramas. The best plays of the period, Hugo's *Hernani* and *Marion Delorme*, Dumas's *Antony*, Vigny's *Chatterton*, seem dreadfully melodramatic to the modern spectator who has the misfortune to see them revived. They all culminate in the cry: "Death to society! Death to reaction!" while bearded young men swing daggers, or pale and white-robed ladies empty the poison cup. Yet the contemporary public liked the performances and applauded heartily. It recognized behind the exaggerated histrionics a new spirit which sought freedom from cant and tradition, and a new independence of the human heart. Never had there been such hatred of the bourgeois as among those young Romantic intellectuals and artists. The drawings and etchings of Gavarni and Daumier still give proof of it. The *épicier* (grocer), the small tradesman, became the symbol of petty egotism and materialism, and, of course, like the Jew in modern times, proved an easy target for an undirected public hatred.

There is a drawing by Gavarni showing a ragged beggar blowing smoke from a cigarette into the face of a passing bourgeois. "Rascal!" cries the bourgeois. "By all means," retorts the vagabond, "anything but an *épicier!*"

Groups of young artists banded together at night and serenaded peaceful citizens, breaking windows and scaring dogs and cats. The bourgeois—the pet child of Louis-Philippe—stood for everything ordinary, conformist, traditional, reactionary. The Romantics thought themselves "different," "superior," "singular." They wanted anything but conformism. They wished to set free the powers of imagination and sensibility, give free vent to individual passion, and display unbridled enthusiasm for everything great, noble, and extraordinary. Passion must rule supreme, for to be passionate meant to be virtuous and generous as well. War had to be waged against anything and anybody who hampered the glorious freedom of the individual—against society, Church, and state.

In their private lives the Romantics proved themselves men by drinking unlimited amounts of beer and rum and by smoking pipe after pipe of tobacco. The latter was even accepted in the salons of the more conventional society matrons who had learned that tobacco-smoking went with progressive views. George Sand in her early novels never forgot to mention that the hero was an ardent pipe-smoker. If alcohol and nicotine were slow in producing ecstasy one took to drugs—opium, morphine, hashish, and stramonium datura. The druggists of Paris were frequently sold out of these items. And there were other ways in which the young Romantics showed themselves contemptuous of death and decay: at various dinners a skeleton was placed at the head of the table and made to talk with the help of a ventrilo-quist. Dumas *père* gave a much-talked-about dinner at which he ate cream out of a human skull.

The fashions hastened to live up to the unconventionality of the day. The streets of Paris were filled with people in queer attire; medieval berets, Spanish capes, and the most extravagant ties and vests were the vogue. Trousers were very narrow and sometimes green, purple, or lavender, to harmonize with the coat lining. Waistcoats were orgies of color and line, and Gautier, of highest rank in Romantic literature, by his red vest became the ultimate expression of daring and sophistication.

The Romantics of the 30's even created their own physi-cal type: the schizophrenic—pale, thin, lemon-colored, and exhausted. The more cadaverous or bilious a person looked the more he approached the beauty standards of the day. It was dreadful to be blond: everyone tried to be dark-haired and olive-skinned, like a true exotic. Hair and beards were dyed, and the latter encouraged to grow with pomades and grease. Vinegar and lemon and a meager diet made up the daily menu of the true Romantic, to promote a languid, anemic air. Women, however, in spite of their ethereal aspect, had to be passionate and display the proverbial ardor and temperament of a Spanish dancer. If they were pale, they were pale from an overabundance of passion, and if they looked exhausted, their eyes must nevertheless be sparkling. The sparkle, if not natural, could be produced by swallowing belladonna.

Interiors of houses were in harmony with these lemon-skinned specters. Furniture stressed the macabre. Rooms had to have "a smell of cemeteries and mortuary vaults." The color schemes of curtains, rugs, and upholstery were dark and severe. Paintings must present massacres, vampires, ruined cloisters, and the witches' sabbath. Gardens were planted with cypresses and evergreens.

And in the midst of this setting worthy of an undertaker's establishment stood the young Romantic, disillusioned, desperate, bored, and with a sense of being completely misunderstood. Discontented with everything, he insisted that nature was in no better mood than he himself and that the frogs in their ponds sighed when they croaked and the mountains would yawn if they could.

Why the bitterness, the ever-ready allusions to death and disintegration? Was it because the Romantic's sensibility was more highly vibrant than others', that his imagination was a richer, more fertile and vivid one? Did he dream too much and in the end awaken to the sterility of this eternal dream? Did he have a horror of reality and forever try to escape from it?

Flaubert, at nineteen, said: "There is no more spring in my heart." Lamartine, describing in a letter his outwardly happy life, continued: "In spite of all this glamour and imaginative power I am the black point where things get dark when they converge. Life is short, empty, has no to-morrow, no interest." Vigny has left us a phrase that sounds like a stoic's epitaph: "Hope is the greatest of all follies." And Musset confessed: "Pleasures cannot help me. I find nothing but such deep disgust that I wish to die. I am sad, ill-humored, tired, exhausted. My stomach is sick. Every-thing bores me." Towards the end of the decade they became as bilious as they looked and had to go to Vichy. Suicides were common and many of the young iconoclasts, if they did not drink themselves to death, died insane and poverty-stricken. "There had been too much dreaming in empty space," said one of them.

All this extravagance was of course not born in a single day. It had its slow evolution and harked back, like Aurore's early emotions on the road to La Châtre, to Rousseau. "Ro-manticism was really born under the former regime, with-out revelation or manifesto; it began with Jean-Jacques, continued with Bernardin, then Chateaubriand and Ma-dame de Staël, and last but not least with the sad and intelli-gent Sénancour." Hugo and his generation felt the full climax of forces which for more than fifty years had pre-pared the advent of the omnipotent and omniscient Roman-tic soul. They were drunk not only with love and poetry but with their own importance, until in the end they shrank in disgust from their inflated egos.

Later most of them were to learn the democratic implica-tions of their liberty, to turn towards the masses and become social-minded. Poets would strive to be politicians and wish to be leaders of men. For the moment, however, they were nothing better than a band of serenaders whose midnight caterwauling was breaking into their contemporaries' peace-ful dreams.

CHAPTER SIX

The Dream Begins

AURORE had been sleeping for an hour or so when her stage finally thundered across the cobblestones of the Paris coachyard. Pale, with distraught features and rumpled clothes, she alighted from the coach almost into the arms of Jules Sandeau, who greeted her with a radiant: "Welcome to Bohemia!"

Sandeau, delicate little twenty-year-old Sandeau, was not the only one of her friends from Berry whom she expected to find in Paris. Many of the young men from La Châtre, to whom Aurore had been hostess in Nohant, were now studying or doing business in Paris: Duvernet a lawyer; Fleury attempting politics; Papet the business man; and others. They were all at her feet, none had escaped her gentle dominance. For Aurore at the age of twenty-six had developed into a woman of mysterious charm and beauty. Her dark melancholy seemed to cover unknown depths of imagination, caprice, and will. The nuns at the convent of the English Sisters used to call her "Sleeping Water." Well, the water was rippling now, whirling, betraying undercurrents of good and evil, sweetness and bitterness. Half angel, half demon, she promised an uncommon career in which no experience would be excluded, except the trite and the banal.

For this young woman stepping from the country stage was no longer the model pupil of the convent nor the quiet, delicate wife of Monsieur Dudevant. She was already "Lélia" of the marble brow, bearing on her forehead the demonic signs of genius and satanic pride. She was already George Sand, whose works, according to the individual temperament of her readers, were to delight, charm, or disgust; in any event confuse. And Lélia had not come to Paris only for a career. She had come to find her complement in the great struggle of the sexes, to find her poet, her Sténio— in a word, she had come to find Sandeau.

Even in Nohant he had more or less been her pet—this young provincial dandy whom the ladies of La Châtre watched blushingly from behind their curtains as he passed by. In those early days Aurore had written him half jestingly, half amorously: "Little Sandeau, graceful and amiable humming-bird of the savannas! Since you left us our cheeks grow pale and our curling-irons rust in the drawers. Your departure means total darkness, like the well-known Egyptian plague."

But here in Paris she would have him for herself, the humming-bird, the dandy of La Châtre who bowed half bewildered, half carried away, to this goddess: "Welcome to Bohemia!"

"Welcome, my poet, my brother, my lover!"

Before long they were sharing an apartment on the Quai Saint-Michel, and the great apprenticeship in love and literature began. Aurore's monthly allowance of two hundred and fifty francs was not enough to keep the lovers in these

exciting times, so they tried to earn money by writing arti·
cles for *Le Figaro*, which had recently been taken over by a
countryman of theirs, de Latouche. De Latouche paid seven
francs a column. Together with Sandeau and Papet, Aurore
spent eight hours daily at the office of *Le Figaro*, her desk
and foot-rug near the fireplace so that unsatisfactory work
could immediately be thrown to the flames. As her first
month's earnings amounted to eighteen francs, much of her
work must have gone up in smoke.

Aurore and Sandeau soon agreed that there was no
money in journalism. With touching eagerness they settled
down at their own little table in their attic on the Left Bank,
and tried to collaborate on a novel. Aurore wrote to one of
her friends: "More than ever I am determined to make a
career of literature, in spite of the revulsion I feel at times,
in spite of the laziness and exhaustion which hamper my
work. My fate seems set: I have a task, a goal, let's quietly
admit—a passion, for writing is a passion."

As a minor gesture towards emancipation Aurore dressed
in men's clothes; this, however, was less singular than it
sounds. Many women did so in her day. It was often the
only way to overcome the difficulties of travel, or of walking
on unpaved streets. In Aurore's case, it was a necessary
economy. Women's skirts were a hazard in the Paris streets
of a hundred years ago. "I was like a ship on the ice, my
thin shoes were torn in two days, the high heels made me
stumble. I never learned to raise my skirts properly. I got
dirty and tired, caught cold, and saw with despair how my
clothes quickly deteriorated and my velvet hats were ruined
by every shower."

She did not look very queer in her male disguise. Her
long overcoat almost covered her ankles; her flying tie and
the gray high hat, tipped a little to one side, looked natural

GEORGE SAND, DRESSED AS A MAN
(Musée Carnavalet)

enough on her. Her heavily nailed boots made walking safe on the cobblestones and the warm coat was an adequate protection against wind and rain.

Sometimes she went hungry, but her head teemed with images and ideas. Better still—she could do as she pleased. Nobody knew her, nobody criticized her, nobody whispered behind her back. She could go and come as she wished, go home through the Luxembourg or along the boulevards; could dine at two or at five, and nobody would ask: "Why? What the devil is on your mind now?"

Yet she was not alone, not abandoned. She had a friend waiting at home, a friend ready to love her, to share madness, enthusiasm, work, and sorrow—a friend with whom she could watch the towers of Notre Dame rise out of the morning mist and the roof of the Louvre sink into darkness at night; a friend who helped her to forget the world and an unpleasant husband. "Life is wonderful, ravishingly sweet in spite of all worries, husbands, burning sorrow. Life is ecstasy! And to love and be loved is heaven brought to earth!"

Whatever her husband might have to say about her present ways did not interest her. Her mother, who had inquired into her life, was told that after all Casimir too did as he pleased. "He has mistresses, or not . . . drinks water or wine, economizes or squanders, builds, plants, changes, buys, directs his estate and business according to his pleasure. I cannot do anything about it, so the least I should be granted is equal independence."

In May she fetched her three-year-old daughter Solange to Paris. Life in the garret on the Quai Saint-Michel was an idyl. Two caged siskins sang in the window. And gradually the vanguard of Paris celebrities came to see the lovers in their retreat near the sky. One of the first was Balzac.

His pockets stuffed with manuscripts, he came puffing into the room, exchanged a few polite words, then impatiently turned to his one and only obsession, his latest book. He read from the novel, then after a while questioned Aurore: "How do you like this chapter, Madame? And you, little one?"

Solange, sitting at his feet, enjoyed it, because it meant that one or more of the funny little sheets might flutter towards her and could be torn into a thousand small scraps.

Shaking his leonine head he would hold forth: "You see, Madame, the difference between your art and mine is this: you describe life as it ought to be—I describe it as it is. But perhaps you are right, too. Go on—idealize, show the pretty and the sweet. That is woman's task anyway."

He would then try to read on until Aurore stopped him with a cry: "Oh, be silent, unfortunate man, if not for my sake, then for the sake of my innocent child! It's obscene. vile, unbearable what you have written there."

The master, furiously stuffing his manuscript sheets back into his wide pockets, turned to go. "And you, Madame, are a fool and a prude!"

Outside on the landing, however, he generally calmed down. "Well, anyway, don't forget to come for supper tomorrow, you and your poet. We will celebrate my new apartment. You will be surprised to see it—all lace and blue silk. And there are two new Chinese vases I must show you. You will be delighted by their beauty, more than by the food I shall have to offer. You will get boiled beef and melons. Do you like melons? . . . Anyway, it is a true Romantic's diet. Good-by, my dear."

At the beginning of the summer months Aurore returned to Nohant for economy's sake, but before leaving Paris she and Sandeau had finished their novel *Rose et Blanche*. They decided to publish it under the pseudonym Jules Sand. Collaboration had been more difficult than they had expected. The plot hung together like poorly glued furniture. Nevertheless, they hoped for the best.

At Nohant, Aurore wrote another novel—this time without Sandeau's assistance. She signed it with the slightly altered pseudonym George Sand, and published it during the winter of 1831–32. It immediately secured her full acknowledgment as a writer, but also roused much controversy. The novel was *Indiana*.

CHAPTER SEVEN

The Humming-Bird in the Fire

WHEN *Indiana* was written, the "social question" had not yet entered the catechism of the Romantics. They were still busy fighting any moral restraint that might be in opposition to their personal passions and desires. Also *Indiana* is rather the child of Chateaubriand than of Rousseau. "If you want to explain everything in this book," George Sand says in her foreword, "take Indiana as a type; she is the woman, the weak being, and represents the repressed passions or rather the passions that the law has prohibited. She is Volition at odds with Necessity; she is Love bruising its forehead against the obstacles erected by civilization. But just as the serpent uses and breaks its teeth trying to bite on steel so the soul's strength exhausts itself trying to conquer life's positivity."

Indiana, ill-mated, leaves her elderly husband for a polite and conventional lover who abandons her almost at once. Repudiated by her husband and the world at large she leaves the country and lands on the Ile de Bourbon, followed

by her faithful English suitor Ralph. Tired and disillusioned, they both try to commit suicide but at the last moment
find a better solution for their problems. In the midst of the
enchanting beauty of the island they settle down to love and
happiness.

Raymon, the unfaithful lover, has a vague likeness to
Aurélien, the smug representative of polite society. As Aurore explains him, he stands for the false logic and the false
morality that govern society. He is the man of honor. He
has the world with him, of course. Does he not sacrifice his
own happiness and personal desires on the altar of conventions? Yet, says George, these conventions are a sham and a
lie, for the morals and principles of society have been made
law only to protect the selfish interests of the ruling class,
just as the clergy instituted cult and dogma in order to in-
sure power and prestige. Laws, however, battle in vain
against the power of love. "No human creature can command love, and nobody is guilty who feels love and loses it
again. Marriage is a human institution but love is of divine
substance."

George felt that her role as plaintiff was inspired by God.
She was pleading the cause of love and humanity under divine direction. Nor is the cause she pleads an insignificant
one : it affects the whole of mankind. "The unhappiness of
woman implies that of man, just as the misfortune of the
slave reflects on his master." In other words, if man had had
his revolution so must woman have hers. Woman too must
assert her human rights and dignity, she must be allowed
to determine her own destiny. She needs space and freedom
—not only the woman of genius, as Madame de Staël
thought, but every woman.

This was the call of Schlegel and Brentano in Germany,
who had tried to liberate women in regard to love and pas-

sion. France had thus far resisted this appeal, but George, at her desk in Nohant, was ready to rip open with her pen the narrow ceiling of woman's universe and let in the sunshine. Society—polite society—responded at once with threats and anathema. The nice people were scandalized and accused the author of being a follower of Saint-Simon, who preached free love with a disintegrating effect upon womanly charm and morals. They did not yet know that the mysterious author, Monsieur George Sand, was a woman, a member of their own social set, who not only preached but practiced her daring doctrine. George had little to say to their objections. When they complained that the iniquity of *Indiana* went unpunished, she said laconically that justice was done only in the melodramas of the boulevard theaters.

Ultimately *Indiana* was a great success. De Latouche said with tears in his eyes: "Oh, my child, I am content with you!" Gustave Planche, the famous and most feared critic of the *Revue des Deux Mondes*, gave a long, favorable report on the book. The newspapers and magazines united in their praise of the new literary star.

Aurore's nearest friends and relatives were less delighted than overcome. Heavens, where had she got all this? How did she happen to breed so much rebellion? At Nohant she had seemed a rather quiet, almost dull little person. But Aurore gave them no answer. She was not a talker, though always an excellent listener. Brain and heart were like delicate antennae, ready to register the vibrations and thoughts of her environment. She might not always clearly formulate what she received, yet she could always make it felt.

The following spring she published two more novels, *Valentine* and *Métella*, for which she was paid three thousand francs each. The new reputation began to pay. *Valentine* was better than *Indiana*, at least by present-day standards. The brilliant description of the Berry countryside will delight readers of literature in any age. She gives us the tortuous little country roads where the carriage just squeezes through with branches of hawthorn gently touching its leather top; she gives us the green depths of woods and valleys; the tall grass of the meadow exhales sweet perfume, the insects hum, and the quail calls in the furrowed field.

But the story itself again attacks ill-assorted unions. The heart, not the pocketbook or the conventions of society, must dictate the young people's choice. Interesting in this novel is the personality of Benedict, if only for the reason that he personifies the true Romantic hero. George goes to great length to describe him, first as to his outer appearance: "He was not without beauty . . . his skin had a bilious pallor, his locks had no color, but his forehead was high and very pure . . . his eyes, with pupils swimming in white and vitreous enamel, had an expression which roused curiosity but they would have brought to nothing all of Lavater's science: they seemed to read deeply in others, but their immobility grew metallic when an indiscreet examination threatened to penetrate them."

This young bourgeois of peasant stock is of course definitely bored with his existence. "Boredom, this terrible evil which is the curse of the present generation, had taken hold of Benedict's destiny in the flower of his youth; like a cloud it covered up his future. It had killed the best faculty of his age—the power to hope!"

He had no occupation. "He had specialized in nothing, dabbled in art and science, but discontinued his studies whenever practical application became necessary. When others collected the fruits of their works he felt disgusted. He never had enough steadfastness to apply the treasures of art and science once he had conquered them, so that they

could serve his actual interests." Benedict, like his contemporaries, like the man who was soon to poison George's life
for a number of years, was always ready to run beyond his
own goals, to idolize his passing enthusiasms, and to spoil
his joys by their very excess.

But the heroine Valentine loves him. "Love is a sentiment which does not calculate or reason. The human heart
receives it from above to project it without hesitation on the
creature chosen by a divine plan; and when an energetic
soul has received this gift, not all mankind can turn it away
from its choice."

This time, however, George listened to public opinion
and let sin find its due and sinister reward. Valentine and
Benedict cannot rejoice in their illegal love because fate in-
tervenes in the form of a jealous suitor who kills Benedict
just when he is free to marry Valentine.

Like *Indiana*, the book is a fair picture of the chaotic
yearnings of the contemporary generation, and the public
hailed it accordingly. If we do not like its standards of male
beauty, if we condemn many of its rebellions as puerile, we
must not overlook the terrific pressure exercised in all direc-
tions by the conventions of the day. There is no doubt that
the reaction was a healthy one, even if it shot past the target
and hit the ridiculous.

The success coming in the wake of *Indiana* and *Valentine*
resulted in an offer from the editor Buloz for George's collaboration on his *Revue des Deux Mondes*. He also contracted for her future works at a higher price. De Latouche,
her former publisher, was much embittered at this treacher-
ous move. But George could easily renounce the *Figaro*,
which had a not very brilliant reputation, in favor of the
Revue, which was the gathering-point of everything important in French literature. But now she had to stand a

worse loss than *Le Figaro* and de Latouche's friendship. It was Sandeau, the smiling and fragrant humming-bird of the savannas, who had unfortunately proved a crow of the common field and wood variety. One day when George returned home unexpectedly, she found him in the arms of a laundress.

The shock was rude, but George shed no tears. Neither did she forgive. Sandeau was expelled from the garret and nothing could make George take him back, even when he lost his hair and took morphine in his grief. He sadly departed for Italy with a knotty stick and a knapsack in his hand and three hundred francs in his pocket. Later, when they are both old and Sandeau is fat and several times a grandfather, they will occasionally meet and bow coldly. And when somebody remarks to Sandeau: "That woman's heart is a cemetery," he will retort: "A cemetery? You mean a necropolis!"

CHAPTER EIGHT

Desire against Truth

THE love affairs of that literary age were apt to end with a *bon mot*, but the irony covered despair rather than indifference. George Sand and Sandeau suffered much from their first great disillusionment. George, in spite of her new-won fame and the financial success which relieved her of much anxiety, felt lonely and abandoned. The year of passion with Sandeau was not so easily forgotten, whatever her pride might say. It seemed but yesterday that she had held her gentle boyish lover in her arms, fearful "lest her passion might burn him to ashes"—yesterday that they had lived, worked, and laughed together. Like Philemon and Baucis, bound together for eternity.

George had moved to a new and larger apartment on the Quai Malaquais, and here her friends came to see her with good advice and consolations. But at night she was alone again. Then she shut herself in "with my inkstand, Solange, the grand piano, and the burning fireplace." She sat at her writing-desk, wrapped in a dark dressing-gown, slippers on her feet, and the eternal cigarette in her mouth.

Her literary success continued. She wrote *La Marquise*, which was well liked, and she told Buloz that he would have to pay four thousand francs for her next book. She wrote easily and fluently, for long hours during the night, never stopping, never tiring, machine-like, as if in a trance. She never reread her work and left the necessary corrections to her publisher. But she could no longer write from a full joyous heart. "My heart is sad and work has become a necessity."

The year 1832, which saw her break with Sandeau, continued to be a Saturnian one. Louis-Philippe discontinued his liberal policy and withdrew into a fog of reactionary measures. Casimir Périer had become prime minister, and his iron-handed methods ruled. A month later the cholera epidemic commenced and the streets of Paris were filled with funeral processions. Thousands died. George was momentarily attacked, or thought herself attacked. Her male friends kept watch at her sickbed and rendered capable assistance, but neither her mother nor any female friend or relative put in an appearance. After a few days she recovered.

In the late spring the plague was over, its last victim the energetic Périer. For a moment the liberals rejoiced, but Périer's successor was Guizot the "Calvinist," who continued the new reactionary policy of the crown. The progressive elements of the country realized that economic rather than political measures were needed to save the country from disaster. But their advice left the king unconvinced and it was years before some sort of social legislation could be enacted.

Nobody seriously considered the welfare of the working people, that is, the whole body of citizens who, in Louis

Blanc's words, possess no capital and no instruments of labor and are therefore dependent on others for the prime necessities of life—the so-called fourth estate. As late as the Year Eleven of the great French Revolution a law had been passed instituting the *livret*—a work-pass for laborers (similar to the one which National Socialist Germany has enacted). No employee could change his place of work without his employer's written permission and testimonial. It practically enslaved the working-man, for it made him powerless to leave his position against his employer's will. Not before 1841 was the first protective law for labor to be passed.

In the meantime the bourgeoisie embarked on a course of pure self-interest. An era of materialism began which had never before been equaled. The big bankers dictated government policies and the slogan of the day was "Enrich yourselves!" For the first time in history money began to obliterate whatever difference in caste there might have been before. Society was divided into two classes—the haves and the have-nots. The steam engine, which became the bourgeoisie's great confederate, helped to build huge fortunes for the few and enslave the large army of employed who were unprotected by legislation. Even the rights of association and strike were taken from them.

The new social theories that sprang up in these problematic times were immediately tabooed by the upper classes, who wanted to keep the status quo, not seeing that it would ultimately draw them into an abyss of unrest and confusion. Proudhon's terrible motto, "Property is theft!" was laughed off, and Saint-Simonism—the strongest social movement of the time, advocating "the physical, moral, and spiritual evolution of the most numerous and poorest class"—was smothered not only by the bourgeois opposition but by in-trigues and incompetency in its own ranks.

Art—but art had not kept its promises either! George said that its atheism had soiled its own cradle. "The time knew only irony or terror. All had become unbelievers, some from dread, others from doubt. My own religiousness had not yet crystallized into socialism to help me in the bat-tle against the terrible breakdown that introduced the era of materialism; and my republican and socialistic ideas were not yet strong enough to illuminate the darkness that Mam-mon spread over the earth. I was left with the image of a God without love, who abandoned humanity to its iniquity and its delusions."

During her long nightly vigils George ruminated over this discouraging truth, and her restless pen turned it into another piece of literature under the title of *Lélia*.

Lélia is less a novel than a series of loosely connected epi-sodes and dreamy speculations. The dreams and desires, the illusions and delusions of George's epoch found expression here in allegorical form. Lélia represents the spiritual urge of the time, Pulchérie, her sister, sensuality and epicurean-ism; Sténio is the enthusiasm and the atony of the artistic soul; Trenmor, stoicism and patience in suffering; Magnus is corrupted faith. All these persons charged with mysterious meaning perform a tragedy of confusion and despair before a truly romantic setting: graves, weeping willows, ruined cloisters, ravines, rocks, and the boiling sea. Secret societies, Utopian kingdoms, ghosts, saints, angels, and madmen have their little corner in this book. George was somewhat reluc-tant to have *Lélia* published. She asked Sainte-Beuve, the critic: "Don't you think it's too fantastic, too incoherent, too much a product of my dreams, for the public to like it?"

But Sainte-Beuve was overwhelmed by the depth and variety of the book's philosophic content. He told George: "It will be your philosophic credo; it will contain your views on life and the world. All your later novels will win in clarity and emphasis by it; this would otherwise have taken much more time." He probably meant that it was good that she had let off steam.

He had real admiration for *Lélia*, however. He thought it incomprehensible, astonishing, that this young woman of twenty-nine could so rapidly and thoroughly light up the furthest and darkest corners of the human mind. "Ah, Madame, yours is a strong and noble soul. Whatever acid the cup may have contained, the metal has remained virginal and uncorrupted."

Sainte-Beuve advised Buloz to publish a chapter from *Lélia* in his *Revue des Deux Mondes*. Though he liked the book he was perhaps uncertain as to its reception. Yet he must have realized that the times, with their despair, their pessimism, their "*mal du siècle*," needed a book like this which might act as a safety valve for the general mental pressure. He must also have realized that *Lélia*, with its vague idealism, would cause a greater repercussion than a more clearly formulated radicalism, which would never have passed the official censor.

Lélia was more than romance and rebellion. It was the Romantic soul struggling in the darkness of its own inflated individualism. "For ten thousand years I have asked the Infinite for truth! Truth! For ten thousand years the Infinite has replied: Desire! Desire! O despairing sibyl! O silent Pythia! Let your head be smashed against the rocks of the cavern and your boiling blood be wed to the roaring sea, for you meant to own the divine truth and yet searched for it ten thousand years in vain!" And Lélia, who tried so long to find God and encountered only the devil—Lélia, who traversed the abyss of extreme human pain and lost the talisman of redemption—dies—at least in the first version of the book—alone on a rock, with the storm roaring around her. But many hundred pages of print were needed to describe the final crisis.

The public lost its head over the book. Youth acclaimed and venerated it. The Church put it on the Index. *Lélia* was a battle-cry and set parents against children, teachers against pupils, Romantics against Realists. Planche, the critic of the *Revue des Deux Mondes*, and Capo de Feuillide, of the *Europe Littéraire*, fought a duel over it. The excitement swept as far as Germany, where "many imitation Lélias were born in the novels of the Countess Hahn-Hahn, in Waldau's *Nach der Natur* and Gutzkow's *Wally, die Zweiflerin*" (Karénine).

The pragmatists tell us that the value of an idea must be measured by the creative unrest it engenders. But it was agitation rather than creative unrest that emanated from *Lélia* as well as from other Romantic works—an agitation which fed the fever of the day or what the literati called the "century's sickness." For the Romantics were not so much concerned with creating something new as with analyzing their own personal discontent and despair, though this discontent and despair might be considered fertile soil for the future creation of a social conscience.

Lélia too is concerned with her personal woes—that vague melancholy and discouragement which eventually develop into despair. "There are hours during the night when I am filled with maddening grief. At first it is a vague sadness, an inexplicable discomfort. The whole cosmos seems to weigh me down and I am a dwarf with the task of a giant. In such moments I need comfort and pity and with childish affection wish to embrace the universe; but the universe rejects and threatens me as if I, an atom, had tried to offend it with my call for help. Then I hate the eternal beauty of the stars and the splendor of nature, which I loved to contemplate—I hate them as the weak man hates the mighty whom he knows to be filled with cold indifference. I hate all creation, and my soul trembles and weeps at nature's bosom like a musical string that breaks in the midst of the divine instrument's most triumphant melodies."

But George Sand's was also the grief of the Romantic who cannot live without his curse. "Don't you know," she told Sainte-Beuve, "that I cannot live without my pain, for it excites and stimulates my jaded nerves? From its convulsions I derive the strength to struggle and to curse. Those who want to die in lethargy know nothing of death's voluptuousness."

And because she wanted pain she needed love. A life without passion was torture to the true Romantic soul, and George, as a Romantic and a woman, felt her loveless existence as a twofold hell. All her energies sought to spend themselves in sentiment and affection—even the universe became an object of desire.

"Oh, Sténio!" says Lélia. "Have you never wept for love of the white stars that adorn the night's blue veil? Did you never kneel to them and stretch your arms towards them and call them sister?"

Ah, to love someone! George tried an affair with the writer Mérimée, the cool and cynical man of the world. His mental superiority had impressed her. Who knew? He might master her wild soul, "for," as she said, "my freedom was killing me."

The affair proved a frightful blunder. Instead of sym-

pathy and understanding Mérimée offered irony and de-
rision. Mérimée wanted a sensuous hour, George a life of
divine love. Within a week the affair was over. George shed
tears of disgust and pain, but dared tell the whole story to
Sainte-Beuve only after five months.

Sainte-Beuve had practical advice. Why not try Alfred
de Musset?

Musset? George shrugged her shoulders. She had met
this twenty-three-year-old hero of Paris society at a literary
dinner. His blond hair, the full red lips, the slim young
body with its eagerness for life seemed charming enough,
but his dandified exterior, the carefully brushed and curled
hair, disgusted her. She suspected behind the lashless, in-
flamed eyes both vanity and sensuality. "No, I don't like
Musset. He is too much the dandy. We would not suit each
other."

It was May 1833 when George put Musset disdainfully
aside; in August they were lovers. Not that he had changed
his character in so short a span of time. He was the type of
the golden youth of 1830—dandy and man of the world.
He gambled, drank, and "assorted with persons of ill-
repute." His elegant figure could be found wherever pleasure and life concentrated: at the Boulevard de Gand, at the
Café de Paris, at the Théâtre Français and the Opéra. As a
member of the French aristocracy he had entry to the most
exclusive circles of society, but he did not refuse to mingle
with its dregs. Money he had none; his patrimony had long
since been spent. Debts were paid by his mother or his publisher, who rarely received anything in return. Virtuous
persons found him rather obnoxious. And yet behind his
ambiguous façade was hidden a human soul full of secret
nostalgia for God.

"Malgré moi l'infini me tourmente."

When George first bound herself to him his genius was still radiant enough to attract her and make her aware of his divine aspirations. They were akin, she felt. And the two poets—god and goddess with feet of clay—threw themselves into each other's ardent embrace for better or for worse.

CHAPTER NINE

Desire against Desire

THEIR union had been preceded by a short literary
skirmish. Musset had written a poem inspired by that
scene in *Indiana* where Raymon spends a night with Noun,
the maid and foster-sister of Indiana, and while in the arms
of the servant longs for the mistress. George sent him the
first volume of *Lélia*, with the dedication: "To my naughty
boy Alfred—George!" and the second volume, with the
words: "To the Count Alfred de Musset in respectful devotion, George Sand." Their conversation was at first on the
level of good fellowship. But in his bare little studio Alfred suddenly changed his mind and discovered that he
loved George—loved her like a mother, a sister, a mistress,
in spite of the difference in their ages (George was six years
older than he), in spite of her lack of elegance and manners, in spite of her life in the midst of the most unbearable
Bohemian crowd. Those were mere superficialities behind
which Musset sensed what he needed: a soul like his own,
ardent and thirsting for beauty; a heart yearning to spend

itself in tenderness, and a passionate nature of almost demonic dimensions. At the end of July, he wrote her the following letter:

"My dear George! I must tell you something silly and
ridiculous. Awkward as I am, I prefer writing to you about
it rather than talking it over after one of our walks. I shall
of course regret it later in the day. For you will laugh at me
and declare me a phrase-monger, you will show me the door
and say that I lie: I fell in love with you the first time I
visited you. I expected it would pass, if I came back as a
friend. Your character has many traits that could cure me
of you. In vain have I talked sense to myself, but the moments spent with you are paid too dearly. . . ."

Whatever George's own good intentions might have
been, they were soon overborne by Musset's passionate appeal, and in August they lived in harmony together in
George's apartment on the Quai Malaquais. Musset's verses
went out into the world where an astonished and amused
public could comment on them:

> "*Te voilà revenu dans mes nuits étoilées,*
> *Bel ange aux yeux d'azur, aux paupières voilées,*
> *Amour, mon bien suprême et que j'avais perdu! . . .*
> *Eh bien, deux mots de toi m'ont fait le roi du monde.*
> *Mets la main sur mon cœur, sa blessure est profonde:*
> *Elargis-la, bel ange, et qu'il en soit brisé!*
> *Jamais amant aimé, mourant pour sa maîtresse,*
> *N'a dans des yeux plus noirs bu la céleste ivresse,*
> *Nul sur un plus beau front, ne t'a jamais baisé.*"

Buloz, Planche, Boucoiran, and Papet witnessed their
ecstatic happiness while Alfred's brother Paul hovered in
the background a sinister scavenger, gathering material for

ALFRED DE MUSSET
Pastel by Landelle *(Louvre)*

his book *Lui et Elle*. It later condemned his brother's Romantic muse to the last corners of hell.

The weeks were filled with gaiety and laughter, with childish pranks and masquerade. And Musset's soul sang until—one day he grew jealous of Planche and disgusted with Boucoiran, who made fun of his fastidious mannerisms.

The lovers decided to escape into solitude and go to Fontainebleau. Here, however, George became aware of Musset's difficult character. He began to remember his adventures with other women and to talk about them; his various hallucinations and obsessions came into the open. One night when he dreamed they were rambling through the forest of Fontainebleau, Musset thought himself pursued by a drunken old man, pale and emaciated by debauchery, who seemed to be driven by a demon. In the end Musset recognized himself in the horrid old man, and then the vision disappeared. Was it a warning that his evil ego was anxious to return? Was the honeymoon over and had the poet tired of harmony and peace? Was his need for sharper and darker stimulants in evidence again?

To understand Musset's character one has to place him against the background of his time. Seen through the eyes of a later, scientific generation, he appears to be one of the many neurotics in which the Romantic age abounded; but it is unfair to consider the living, burning, highly sensitive organism of the Romantic as psychopathic only. It is more reasonable to consider him as an individual of surprising breadth of consciousness—an individual whose mind had deepened so far as to allow him to live on more than one level of consciousness. When we read the works of Poe, Novalis, Hoffmann, Victor Hugo, and other poets of the time, we realize that they drew not only upon their conscious but upon their unconscious as well. Most of them experienced hallucinations and artistic visions. The latter held no terror for them. The former—the shadow, the evil genius—was an experience which Musset, Hugo, Hoffmann, and others often described. Some tried by drugs or alcohol to push the limits of the conscious ego far beyond its borders into the realm of the unconscious. The realists of the generation to follow came to speak derisively of "Romantic mysticism," while modern psychology would rather call that condition a mental phenomenon to which we ourselves ought ultimately to aspire—though by more rational means.

Musset, who in his writing was almost a classicist, was emotionally a child of Romanticism. In the truest sense of the word he belonged to the "pale, ardent, nervous, post-Napoleonic generation." As a child he was so impressionable and delicate that his mother dared not punish him even when he cut up the new curtains, smashed the mirror with a billiard cue, and disfigured the family portraits with sealing wax!

In his *Confessions of a Child of the Century* he describes his unbalanced moods in the following way: "Some days I was in such a bizarre frame of mind that it is hard to describe it. In the morning I woke exhausted without cause, as after a great debauch. All outward impressions tired me, all familiar things bored or disgusted me; what I or others had said the day before I ridiculed now. Unable to move, I remained on my couch and designedly changed all plans made the day before; it amused me to recapitulate the tender words I had had for my mistress the day before and to poison them now by jeering and irony."

He had taken Byron for a model and went in for heavy drinking. He liked a concoction of beer and rum, and according to his friends drank mathematically, gravely, increasing the amount in proportion to the depth of his mental depression. When he had drunk himself into a stupor he would lie on his couch for hours, still conscious of what went on around him but "visualizing it as from another star."

After the first few weeks George must have realized that Musset did not love her as she expected and that he was probably incapable of a deep and lasting affection. But she clung to the delusion of this love with the obstinacy of a gambler who will not acknowledge that he has once more placed his odds all wrong. She would rather suffer in silence and endure Musset's moods than be alone again.

The severity she had shown in Sandeau's days had left her. Perhaps Musset's finer nature still held her enchanted and made her forget his evil traits. Even in his worst moments he retained some of the poet's divine sweetness. In his blackest fits of temper he still had the beauty of the fallen angel!

And George was young, and to be young meant to will happiness. "That is the essential in all youth: that it wants to find happiness and keep it. If it could resign instead of pursuing with tears, if it would not rise after every fall, if it would not feed on its disappointments, imaginations, burning faith, radiant enthusiasm, ire, and disgust—on its triumphs as well as its defeats—youth would not be youth!"

Paris society took an active interest in the development of the amorous adventure; wagers were placed in the smart salons for or against its continuation. On the whole the union between the gifted pleasure-bent boy and the older headstrong woman was judged skeptically.

To escape the general gossip, perhaps to give new strength to a waning emotion, the couple resolved on a trip to Italy. Buloz, their publisher, must advance the necessary funds. Maurice, George's ten-year-old son, was to remain in his Paris school; Solange with a reliable nurse was sent back to Nohant. One painful task remained: to ask Madame de Musset *mère* for permission to let her son travel south.

It was a difficult interview; Musset had not enough courage to go himself; he sent George. Heavily veiled, Madame Sand called on the surprised and somewhat helpless Madame de Musset to explain the situation. "Madame, trust your son to my hands! I shall be like a mother to him. I guarantee you his safety as if he were my own child!"

Boucoiran was told to close up the apartment on the Quai Malaquais. "Put things carefully away and take the keys of the drawers with you." There was always a chance that Casimir might be tempted to investigate.

George and Musset took the stage to Lyon and then sailed by boat to Avignon. It was December and a cold wind swept down the Rhône, forcing the travelers to huddle around the cabin stove.

There the couple jostled against Henri Beyle (Stendhal), who was returning to his consular post in Civitavecchia. Clad in fur and high boots, the novelist looked ready for an Arctic expedition.

Musset introduced him to George, and while Stendhal with lively gesticulation talked to her of Italy, George contemplated him in silence, "as if he were an unknown species of bug or herb."

"He reminds me of de Latouche," George mused. "He has the same mannerisms when he talks, and there are other resemblances. Beyle's face in spite of its bloated features is spiritual enough. But I don't like his conversation. It

is too brilliant!" While George listened in silence
tried to give her a witty, spirited picture of the Ita
about to see.

"You are looking forward to Italy? You still
sions, haven't you? You will soon lose them. T
are the most boring people in the world, stupid a
Negroes. Books, newspapers, whatever is new a
ing is of no concern to them. You cannot talk t
you don't want any *conversazioni?* You wan
as far as I can see, people who go to Italy for ;
idle fools."

George looked shocked. "He is embittered,"
"because he had to leave Paris." She did not lik
berated her ideals. Quickly she changed the su

The more George saw of Stendhal the less
When he finally managed to get drunk, and
ward bear stalked through the room in his he
lady was through with him. "I am glad he
at Avignon; otherwise I would have left the

After Avignon the two lovers were left to
by the time they reached Genoa their joy in traveling had
yielded to a sense of irritation. Perhaps they were too much
together—always a trial for the hypersensitive.

George suffered a fever attack and showed her famous
"long face." Yet day after day she managed to put in six
hours of work, covering sheet after sheet with her even and
somewhat naïve handwriting. Buloz was clamoring for
copy. Had he advanced his money for nothing?

Musset, however, did not dream of working. "I cannot
produce literature by the yard like you!" he told George.
"I am an artist, not an artisan. Genoa bores me, too. My
imagination goes stale on me here."

George suggested that he visit the balls and *conversazioni*. "Why don't you go and amuse yourself there? Only one thing I beg of you: don't gamble!"

But Musset was bored by society unless he could gamble or court the women. "Both are impossible as long as you are around," he uttered with a sigh, and then added as if to redeem himself: "My God, don't look at me that way. You know that the slightest reproach upsets me. You misuse your power. Don't be surprised if I get suddenly tired of it."

The same scene would repeat itself day after day, and in the end Musset would take his hat and leave the house, banging the door behind him. Finally he told her: "I am sorry, George, I made a mistake. But I don't love you any more." In his *Confessions* he elaborates on this: "I was young and fond of pleasure. This daily tête-à-tête with an older woman who suffered and wore herself out, this face which grew more and more serious as time went on—all this made me rebellious, and I missed my freedom bitterly."

The beauty of the Tuscan landscape did not relieve the strain. George was still ill, yet she continued to visit museums and churches until at night she dreamed that she had turned into a mosaic. "Patiently I counted my little blue and red squares."

Rapidly they passed through Ferrara and Bologna as if —like Paolo and Francesca—they were blown forward by a hellish wind.

In Venice, where they stopped at the Hôtel Danieli, George recovered from her fever spell, but Musset now succumbed. George wrote her Paris friends that he had typhoid fever. This was not true. Whatever it may have been, it was brought on by alcoholic excesses and its final diagnosis was delirium tremens.

For seventeen nights and days George kept watch at his sickbed and nursed the ungrateful child back to health. For had she not sworn to Madame de Musset that she would watch over him like a mother? She was assisted in her task by the young Venetian doctor, Pietro Pagello, who became her principal friend and adviser.

She liked the good-looking young man whose brown eyes promised devotion and faithfulness. While Alfred slept through nights of convalescence, she wrote to Pagello the famous missive which did so much to ruin her reputation:

"To stupid Pagello! You do not know me and I do not know you. I am ignorant of your character, your past, and what people think of you! Perhaps you are the kindest, perhaps the cruelest, of men. I love you without being sure that I can respect you. I love you because something draws me towards you, yet tomorrow I may hate you instead. If you were a countryman of mine I could ask you and you could understand me. But this might make things worse, for you might answer with a lie. But you will tell me no lies. You will make no false promises and swear no false oaths. You will love me as best you can. Maybe you will be incapable of offering me what I have looked for to this very day, but at least I can imagine that you might. Your expression and tenderness I can interpret as I wish and you cannot mislead me with false words. If your glance is tender I shall imagine that your soul converses with me. If you look up to the sky I shall believe that your soul longs for the divine from which it emanates. Don't therefore learn my language and neither will I look for words in yours. Let me remain ignorant of your life. I wish I did not even know your name. Please hide at least your innermost self before me, so that I can forever think it beautiful."

George did not realize that she wrote not to Pagello in

her letter, but to the unknown which so far had been unable to hurt her, and possibly might never hurt her if she left it unnamed. From a pallid reality she escaped into a brand-new artificial heaven where objects remained without power because—oh, magic intuition!—they had no names.

She deceived herself so well she could tell Pagello that Musset meant nothing to her; he was only a sick and extravagant child in her care—a child who had worn her down by his bad behavior.

But Pagello sensed the ambiguousness of George's emotions. He struggled hard—he even sought inspiration from his mother's portrait, before he gave himself up to the new but dangerous muse.

Musset in his feverishness was aware of his mistress's infidelity. There were painful scenes in which Alfred attacked George with a knife, while she threatened to lock him up in an insane asylum. But after his convalescence was well under way, he repented of his sins with tears in his eyes and gave his blessing to George's alliance with Pagello. Calm at last, he left for Paris—alone. George did not dare to accompany him to his first stop, Vicenza (not being too sure of her own emotions). But she rushed down there next day, accompanied by the understanding Pagello, to inquire "how Monsieur de Musset had spent the night." All along the trip Alfred found George's letters full of concern for his health and sleep. "Write to me from every town where you stop for the night. Good-by, angel. May God protect you and bring you back if I am still here. At all events I shall see you during the fall vacation. And how happy we shall be! How we shall love each other, my little child, my brother. Ah, who will nurse you in the meantime and whom shall I nurse? How shall I get on without the good and the evil you mean to me?"

Musset answered with more regrets and sighs: "Oh, I love you still as a lover, George! Yet knowing you near a man you love, I am calm. . . . My poor George, poor dear child. You have deceived yourself. You thought yourself my mistress but you were only my mother." He also assured her that he deserved to lose her and that nothing could be too hard a punishment. But her memory was pure within his heart. Nothing unclean was associated with her image, and he could remember her only with respect, with tears and undying affection.

George answered by return mail: "I know that I love you and that is all. . . . I hear your voice in the silence of the night. . . . I don't remember anything except that we have been very unhappy and that we are separated. . . . One day you reproached me for not giving you any true pleasure in love, but at least you will not think of me when you find pleasure in other women's arms."

Her relationship with Pagello was made light of, as if he were a good friend, helpful but a bit dense. She gave some amusing descriptions of Pagello's former mistress, a fury who tore out his hair and pulled at his coat. The woman came to see George, who then managed to reconcile her to Pagello. The latter really was an angel of virtue. "I pass the sweetest moments of the day talking to him about you."

Poor Pagello, poor Musset, and poor George, trying with subterfuges and half-truths to cover the confusion of their love. George's pride had forced her into Pagello's arms, but she felt very uncomfortable there and longed to get back where she really belonged—into Musset's heart.

Musset was trying to be reasonable. He bought the perfumes and gloves George ordered; he corrected her manuscripts and gave her good advice on her future travels. George had planned to leave Venice and go to Constantinople. She felt too restless to stay on alone. But Musset advised that she finish *André* first, and then save the money instead of spending it on extravagances. His outward calm, his self-possession, were merely a mask. His sister described what he was really like: "When he came back he was more in love than ever and sick, sick, sick, the poor child! He stood before us emaciated and completely changed; half of his hair was gone. He tore it out in tufts."

After a while he confessed to George that he could neither work nor amuse himself. "Six months ago the mild spring air still affected me like champagne and led me, after a good meal, into the arms of the first woman. If at her house I found a couch, friends, and a good cigar, I wished for nothing better. If an hour later in my own room I felt like weeping, I excused my state as due to boredom or nervous excitement. Now, if my senses would take me to a prostitute I am afraid that during the climax I might scream and strangle her."

George took a more sensible course to get over her disillusionment. She started on a walking trip in the Venetian Alps. In men's clothes, with a big stick in her hand, a knapsack on her back, her pockets filled with cigarette papers and tobacco, she rambled along the River Brenta and up into the mountains. Some of the innkeepers had misgivings about this brown-skinned little fellow who looked as if he had run away from school. They locked away their crockery and linen when he was about. In Olivieri George was almost picked up as the accomplice of a crook. She had dined with the man on his orders, afraid to refuse because he looked so ferocious and his stick had frightened her. When he left without paying his bill, she was made responsible and was allowed to go free only after much heated argument.

She returned to Venice with only a few cents in her pockets. Soon her life resumed a smooth course of work and romance. She had rented a house together with Pagello and his brother Roberto; the two men lived on the main floor, while she shared the upper story with their sister. Venice at last smiled on her and she could enjoy nightly gondola rides with moonlight, love, and gay supper parties. During the day she continued to slave at her writing-desk. She wrote the first of her *Letters of a Traveler*, an autobiographical sketch on her life in Venice, and *Jacques*, another novel about marriage. She found time to do needlework. Pagello in his diary tells us that in her moments of leisure she knitted, drew, or embroidered. She sewed curtains for Pagello's brother and knitted half a dozen pairs of stockings for their father. Even her cooking deserved praise, and the artichokes she prepared for dinner were superior to anything Pagello had tasted before. Her economy, her diligence, her excellent cooking made her a veritable jewel in the eyes of the domestic-minded doctor.

Whether George imagined she could become rooted in the lukewarm happiness of her Italian idyl is a question. Yes—Pagello, too, was a Romantic. Before breakfast he would walk miles to find a few flowers for his mistress's dressing table, and when she had no money, because Buloz's checks went astray, he pawned his clothes. But he lagged behind her in power of imagination and warmth, and often stood confused at the ways of her nature, which—vital and creative—projected itself in many unforeseen channels.

Her literary output profited by her calm existence. Besides *Jacques* she wrote *André* and *Leone Leoni*. In all of them we are confronted by the strange reasoning of the true Romantic. Not virtue rules, but passion! Passion, holy or unholy, must run its course and cannot take merit or virtue into consideration.

Leone Leoni particularly undercuts the reader's standards of justice and morality. Though the book is full of murder, gambling, elopements, duels, and reconciliations, the characters and scenes are recognizable, as again and again Musset, the Hôtel Danieli, Pagello, and even Musset's Mephistophelean adviser, Tattet, turn up in the story. None the less, the book made an impression among its readers that sometimes changed their lives—Liszt and the Countess d'Agoult were not the only admirers who under its influence defied convention and broke legal ties.

The first of the *Letters of a Traveler* is a relief after these novels. It is one of the many charming autobiographical essays which Sand herself valued little and grouped together and sold as "journalism." Yet in beauty, clarity, and level-headedness they rank with, and sometimes above, her best fiction.

In July 1834 the episode with Pagello neared its end. The sky had been unfailingly blue and the lagoons so quiet that not even the starlight trembled on their surface. For weeks life had been as dreamless and unproblematical as that of a plant.

Then rose the urge to change this life and drift back north again where colors were less bright, objects less sharply outlined, but where there was the intermittent play of light and darkness, of pleasure and pain, and where unquenched desire relieved the monotone of too much simple bliss.

Pagello accompanied Madame Sand to Paris, since George insisted that the doctor was part of her life. But Pagello, who was a Latin and far more perspicacious, knew better.

For a possible emergency he carried along two famous oil paintings, which could easily be turned into cash.

George arrived in Paris in time to attend the distribution of prizes at Maurice's school and immediately afterward left with her son for Nohant. She had only a short interview with Musset, who found her sympathetic but rather cool. Disappointed by this attitude, Musset left for Baden.

Pagello remained in Paris, in care of Boucoiran and Buloz. He knew his part was over but he utilized his stay in Paris by attending courses at the Charité. After a few months he returned to Italy, where fate held in store for him a kindlier future. He married twice, was happy in both unions, enjoyed an excellent practice, and lived to a ripe old age.

CHAPTER TEN

"And I? What Am I?"

FOR the first time in two years George was home in Nohant. In a way she was happy to be back. Even Casimir seemed amiable, though the Venetian adventure was no secret to him. But George's nerves were frayed and her thoughts in a turmoil. While the autumn moon spread its honey-colored light over the dark park trees she paced the garden paths, Néraud and Rollinat at her sides.

"Yes," she told them with an undertone of irritation, "it is lovely to find you and the children and the gay old rhythm of our former life in Nohant. But in vain do I try to associate myself with it. Perhaps my mind and heart have grown obtuse and numb through false ideas or too adventurous a life. Yet, you see me dying rather than living, and you, my friends, cannot do anything but comfort me before my end."

Books must fill the void of her heart. With much satisfaction she read *The Life of Alfieri* and Madame de Staël's *Thoughts about Suicide*. She did not agree with Madame de Staël, but Alfieri delighted her. "He is a man after my own heart. What I admire is his pride, what thrills me is his terrible struggles between weakness and pride. Oh, this man has suffered much, has learned to despise life, has wept and writhed in convulsions, fighting against his self-destructive instincts."

Pride alone could cure her unhappiness. It was the bubble rising within, showing that there was life in her still. Pride—and death! She wanted to die. Yes, it was nice to resolve to die. One was proud of the idea, because it meant resisting fate and tricking it. It was a very consoling resolution, so consoling that one was almost ready to give it up again after thinking it over. Besides—wasn't it a remedy that a wigmaker and a prostitute might choose as easily as a Cato of Utica?

Nevertheless George felt that she would perhaps die after all. She entered into an agreement with Buloz assuring her daughter a dowry in case of her own premature death. She sold him her memoirs for forty thousand francs; ten thousand she received on account. Musset, the cause of all this confusion, was meanwhile alone in Baden, shut up in a small dingy hotel room where he stared all day at his door, hoping that it might open and his lost love come back to him. "Ah, George, I thirst for you. My love, my life! I hold you against my heart, my wonderful mistress, my first and last love!"

A month later they were both in Paris and like fated meteors rushed toward their last encounter. Almost immediately after the reunion Musset cooled toward her, as if his passion had waited for the one spark that would ignite it and also burn its last reserve. He who had wanted to die for his mistress the day before, now turned away in contempt. George begged him on her knees to receive her at his apartment; she cut off her hair as a sign of her utter

despair. He only shrugged his shoulders at the poor de-
mented creature and joked about her in the presence of his
friend Tattet.

The tortures of those days are written, in true Romantic
style, into George's intimate Journal: "Oh, my blue eyes,
you do not glance at me any more. Your noble head will
never again bow down to me in divine voluptuousness. Your
ardent supple body will not bend over me like Elijah who
restored the sick child to life. Farewell, blond locks, white
shoulders, farewell whatever was mine and that I loved.
On warm nights I shall call your name and go embracing
the trees and rocks of nature to faint on the cold ground
after my desire has been gratified."

In those days Delacroix drew a portrait of her which
shows her pale and thin, with drawn features, uncouth
short hair, and a naïve yet appealing look in her eyes. This
is George, not the impressive Madame Sand who will eventually be proposed for a seat in the Academy; not Lélia the
superwoman who brought chaos into so many men's lives.
One remembers Balzac's verdict: "She is a female bachelor,
she is an artist, she is generous, kind, loyal; she is chaste.
Her best traits are those of a man—morally she is like a
boy of twenty, for in her innermost heart she is pure and
also a prude. . . . Her follies are so many honorary titles in
the eyes of the well-meaning and just."

While she was sitting for her painting at Delacroix's
studio, the artist advised her what to do: to let go, to forget! He said: "When I am in the condition you are in now,
I show no pride; I was not born a Roman. I abandon myself
to despair. It grips, overpowers, gnaws at me, but when it has
enough it becomes exhausted and leaves me in peace."

Whereupon George went home and wrote in her diary:

"What do I care about their theories? . . . I *feel*—that is all! I love! The force of my passion would carry me to the end of the world!"

Sometimes she mused on the fact that she had been the mistress of two men at the same time. Addressing herself to an imaginary Musset in her Journal, she said: "You say: one cannot love two men. Nevertheless it has happened to me. It happened once, it will not happen again. . . . Do I not suffer from my follies and mistakes . . . ? Are lessons of no value to women like me?"

Yet, she was still a young woman capable of giving a man full happiness. But she needed a steadfast hand, a heart without vanity, to receive and sustain her. "If I had found such a man I would not be where I am now."

But on second thought she denied her need of the strong hand: "These masterful men are like gnarled oaks whose exterior is repellent! Also they are brutal. I hate their cowardice and hypocrisy. I hate their smugness. They build a whole system of virtue on their theories of crime."

This was a shot taken at Casimir. But Musset was in for reproach too. "And you poet, lovely flower, your fragrance intoxicated me, poisoned me. You were too suave, too subtle." She likened him to the blossoming shrubs of India and China which sway in every breeze. "From their frail stems we cannot obtain the strong beams necessary to build a home. We taste their nectar, we grow heady with their perfume, and under their influence we fall asleep and die."

She also asked advice of Liszt, who was one of the circle and considered a possible successor to Sandeau, but he answered that God alone deserved to be loved. "It is true," she told her diary. "But when one has loved a man it is very hard to love God. It is so difficult. Liszt also says that the only keen sympathy he ever felt was for Monsieur de Lamennais and he added that earthly love would never take possession of him. He is very lucky—the good little Christian!"

She grew so restless that she preferred playing dominoes at a café all night to staying at home alone. "To be alone —what horror!" she complained to Sainte-Beuve. She promenaded her grief in the studios and cafés of Montparnasse or she went to the Opéra in men's clothes to secure cheaper standing room in the pit. In her sailor hat and heavy coat and boots she felt unhappy now in the midst of all the men in black who were so much bigger and stronger, and jostled and crushed her. She was conscious of her hollow cheeks and eyes that were swollen and red from weeping. With her love of dramatization she confessed: "I looked dull and old. Above me [in the opera boxes] were all those blond women, white and pink, decked out with jewels and feathers, wearing their hair in luxurious curls, carrying bouquets, displaying naked shoulders. And I, what am I, poor George?"

The envy of those charming blondes above her grew more acute as she feared that Fantasio—that is, Musset—would choose his next mistress from among them. "Madman, you are leaving me in the most beautiful mood of my life, in the phase of my love that is most real, most passionate, and most replete with suffering. Oh, what fever, sent by celestial vengeance, burns in my bones! What wrong have I done to be punished by this leonine love I feel within me?"

Again she contemplated escape through suicide, but the thought of her children made her shrink from it. Maurice must not undergo the tortures of her own parentless childhood.

Papet, casting around for someone to divert her, arranged an interview with Sandeau. But when the two former lovers met, they found nothing better to discuss than the disparaging remarks each had been reported to be circulating about the other. Finally they both denied having said anything at all and smoked a cigarette together, George keeping her feet on a hot-water bottle as a sign of her ailing health. Sandeau was sent off with a reminder that they must not meet again, as it might ruin her reputation—mostly in Musset's eyes. But if they should meet, he was to greet her amicably and respectfully. When he had left, the diary received the following entry: "I am comforted by this meeting. When two people have loved each other it is frightful not to remain friends. For good or ill they have loved each other."

When the first fury of her unfulfilled passion had spent itself, she sent her diary to Musset so that he might be convinced of the sincerity of her grief and her love. But Musset was not impressed. His brother said: "His memories of the past, his fatal experience told him that pride was still there disguised beneath the mask of humility." And as far as the "leonine love" was concerned, Musset feared rather than desired it.

Nevertheless, for the time being the manuscript remained in Musset's possession. It was lent by Musset to Madame Jaubert, his "godmother," who when asked to return it stayed up all night with her maid and daughter copying it. The copy was later used by Paul de Musset when he wrote his book *Lui et Elle*. The manuscript itself came back into George's possession only in 1840, when she asked Musset for its return. Musset is said to have been unaware of Madame Jaubert's breach of faith and lack of discretion.

In November 1834 George tried Nohant again, hoping for peace and forgetfulness. Musset wrote her in a sympathetic, forgiving mood. In January she was back in Paris, reconciled with Musset until their final break, which occurred in March. Five years later, when her diary was back in her possession, she penciled at the bottom of the last page: "Heine has precious words. Tonight he said concerning Musset: 'This is a young man with a very promising past.' "

Musset left an account of their relationship in his *Confessions of a Child of the Century*. It betrays pain and regret. "I have written it with my heart's blood," he confessed. George published her version of the story only after Musset's death. Her novel *Elle et Lui* is a clever book, full of keen observation, of realistic phrasing, and even humor! It may not have been written with the old feeling, but there is no way of knowing how long the heart will actually remember its joys and despair. It would be a mistake to infer from the book that George was indifferent to the former conflict between herself and Musset. She had a remarkable capacity for eliminating the negative from her life.

Musset was weaker, perhaps he was more sincere. His poetry and plays, written after the Venice trip, contain many allusions to his greatest love. The memory of those days stayed with him to the last.

> *"Un jour je fus aimé, j'aimais, elle était belle.*
> *J'enfouis ce trésor dans mon âme immortelle,*
> *Et je l'emporte à Dieu!"*

Not in his deeds but in his last word he got the better of George.

PART TWO

The Dream That Was Socialism

*"Ne voyez-vous pas que leurs passions
de politiques sont devenues sociales?"*

—ALEXIS DE TOCQUEVILLE

CHAPTER ONE

Republican Dawn

"WE HAD climbed the unending flights of stairs at No. 18 Quai Malaquais in vain. We were told that Madame was resting; she had been working all night and was tired."

It was Heinrich Heine and August Lewald who had called. The German journalist Lewald, on a visit in Paris, was seeking an interview with Madame Sand and expected to be introduced by Heine, then firmly established as a friend of the famous authoress. "My cousin Heine," George used to call him, proclaiming her kinship to the man whose social background equaled her own in ambiguity. She liked him and when people spoke ill of him in her presence she took up his defense, insisting that he was better than his reputation and had an essentially kind heart.

The two Germans were admitted the following day and Madame received them in what Lewald described as a dark niche, draped like a tent. George was reclining on a couch covered with cushions. She was busy rolling cigarettes.

Lewald saw her as a delicate little woman with large, somewhat protruding eyes. "When she spoke she showed her large white teeth, and her strong aquiline nose lent her an expression of determination which, however, did not impair her feminine grace."

They talked about literature; Lewald mentioned the foremost muses of German Romanticism: Bettina von Arnim and Rahel Varnhagen. George had never heard of them but she inquired after the "kind Mrs. Chézy," a popular German fiction writer who had made herself conspicuous by her strange clothes and manners rather than by her literary accomplishment.

That night Lewald and Heine met George again, at the Opéra. "All the other women had coquettish coifs or broad-brimmed fashionable hats with nodding flower bouquets," noted Lewald. "George alone appeared in the simplest and most natural hairdress in the world. The Republican lawyer Michel [Michel de Bourges], whose only point of elegance was a pair of white gloves, conducted her upstairs, where she turned back toward us for a moment and discoursed in a gay manner."

The time was 1836. A year or more had passed since George had wept over the unfaithful Alfred, and her outlook on life had undergone a certain revision. Lélia—or rather that romantic part of herself that she had projected into Lélia—had died with her love for Musset. "You don't love any more?" Pulchérie had asked Lélia. And the answer had been: "No, and therefore I am dead."

There had been in Lélia—and in George—an excess of Romanticism, too much self-will and passionate emotion, too much of the two great contemporary diseases: love and megalomania. But the former George who had insisted on her individual rights, who had swept aside all moral and conventional restrictions, had gone out of existence and was no more. She had had her life of thrills and public battles, but her attempt at self-realization had led her into the immensity of the desert rather than the immensity of the heavens. The pursuit of individual happiness and freedom, so enchanting at first, had proved sterile, bitter, and heartbreaking.

George wrote in her diary: "Farewell, Eros! You idol of my youth! A last glance and, as a last offering, a wreath of fresh roses to you and then good-by! Look out for happier and younger Levites, insatiable God, for I am no longer among your followers. The past is but a remnant of a torn chain ready to drop off at the first suitable occasion, while the present and future are free for the service of an ideal rather than a personal passion, of humanity rather than an individual."

George looked at the world again and found something better than private worries and ambitions. The times were offering her problems in need of immediate solution, problems bearing on unemployment and disorganized production—so much so that her friends used as a current phrase: "Let's pose the social question!"

Louis Blanc has described the chaotic industrial conditions in his *History of Ten Years*. The producers were struggling for "possession of the market"; the workers were struggling for "possession of employment"; employers fought employees on the question of wages; and the worker fought the machine, which, "by supplanting him, let him starve."

In 1834, 130,000 children were abandoned in the streets. In the Twelfth Precinct of Paris 24,000 people were without food or adequate clothing. In Lyon the weavers' wages had been reduced to ninety centimes (less than twenty cents) for an eighteen-hour day. Brothers begrudged each other the last piece of bread. The general misery and starvation were indicated by the army statistics of those years, which showed that in the industrial centers ninety out of a hundred recruits were unfit for military service.

The free competitive system in commerce and industry threatened havoc in a society that had not yet established a reasonable code of business ethics and ruthlessly undersold its goods whenever necessary. Reaction to such *laissez-faire* policies began to make itself felt in a number of ways.

It is said that Utopias are born of the crises of an age: if the present seems pregnant with catastrophes, there are always theories in readiness to forestall and overcome them. The 30's in France abounded in such theories and remedies. Among the movements toward reform Saint-Simonism was for a time the most popular, as it gave inspiration to the workman, the artist, and the intellectual—all, according to Saint-Simon, destined to be the cornerstones of future society.

Count Henri de Saint-Simon, founder of the doctrine and father of French socialism, was a descendant of a famous line of nobles who had played their hereditary role in French court life for centuries. Born in 1760, Saint-Simon belonged to the generation of Lafayette, Robespierre, and Danton. He believed in the cause of liberalism and earned his first Republican laurels in helping fight the war of American independence. From what he saw in America he signaled the beginning of a new political era. He foretold that the American Revolution would necessarily determine the progress of civilization in general and within a short time would change the entire social order then existing in Europe.

The versatile count—who in the course of his life had tasted of every science, lived on many social levels, helped "more ideas into the world than a doctor could hope to deliver children," and finally settled down to build up a whole new science—was one of those human phenomena who stir people's imaginations through phrases rather than well-thought-out doctrines. Systems he declared to be delusions. "One does not create a system of social organizations . . . one rather observes the new interweaving of ideas and interests that have been formed and tries to demonstrate them. A social system is a fact or it is nothing at all."

He was the first to use the word "industry" and, in his own way, to analyze its content. He advocated an "industrial state" organized for productive labor and representing a threefold hierarchy of artists-priests, scientists, and "industrialists." "Industrialists"—that is, the working-class—were considered the best part of society, though the ruling class still regarded them as proletarians and have-nots. Saint-Simon insisted that the furtherance of their status must be the ultimate effort of society.

Saint-Simon did not touch upon private property, education, or the family. He predicted, however, the coming struggle between the bourgeois and working-classes and the association of all workers. As an ultimate rule for all humanity he demanded that "under all circumstances men must conduct themselves as brothers."

The count's most prominent disciples were Augustin Thierry and Auguste Comte, but the actual school was founded by his intimate companions, Olinde Rodrigues, Bazard, and Enfantin. Using Saint-Simon's most important works as a basis, Bazard formulated a program which contained most of the demands of modern socialism: industrial planning, socialized means of production, unionization of labor, abolishment of inherited property, and equal political and economic rights for all.

Saint-Simonism would probably have become a most effective reform movement had it not been spoiled by mysticism and queer ritual—additions for which "Father" Enfantin was responsible. Enfantin also told his fellow-sectarians: "Become sanctified by work and *pleasure!*" He fought for the full sexual emancipation of women: "Woman shall reveal whatever she feels, whatever she desires. Those who subject women to law are not true Saint-Simonists. The only point of view any Saint-Simonist can hold is to declare himself incapable of judging women ever."

According to Enfantin the social individual was formed by the union of man and woman—the priest-couple. "How beautiful will be their mission! Man and wife! They will know decency and chastity and beauty and voluptuousness!"

Adolphe Guéroult, politician, writer, and disciple of Saint-Simonism, worked hard to convince George of the merits of the creed. He wanted to propose her as the sect's outstanding member and "Mother." The "Mother" George refused, but the membership she accepted, especially after Liszt had urged her to do so. Presents filled her attic in the next three years, representing many loving gifts from her fellow-members. But the paper flowers, lacquered boxes, vases, shawls, and hats amused her children more than herself.

George felt that more effective reforms were about to be accomplished by the Republican party, a conviction for which her lawyer, Michel de Bourges, whom Heine and Lewald had seen by her side at the Opéra, was responsible. From the Republican party George, and with her the liberals of the day, expected the salvation of mankind. "Republic," she exclaimed in one of her letters, "dawn of justice and equality, divine Utopia, sun of a future that may never materialize, hail to you!"

The Republicans held the left wing of the opposition parties under Louis-Philippe, acquiring weight and importance in the years after 1830 when the government failed in its program of reorganization and reform.

The more radical members of the party, realizing the importance of the new industrial development, strove to educate the workman and make him conscious of his rights and potentialities. They organized secret political societies —among them the important one of the Rights of Man— and worked on the proletarian masses of the great French industrial centers much along the programmatic lines of future militant communism. Their means of propaganda included newspapers, pamphlets, political clubs, and agitators. Heine, who had mentioned the existence of these secret societies in the *Gazette d'Augsburg*, feared their power of propaganda and on the other hand called them old-fashioned, because they harked back to the phraseology of 1793. But the secret leader and inspirer of the party was Buonarroti, the famous Carbonaro who had organized the Republican party first in Italy and then in France. He was an old revolutionary battle-ax and a former colleague of Babeuf, with whom he had shared a prison-cell in 1797 for participation in the "Conspiracy of the Equals." As an advocate of Babouvism under the Restoration, he planted the first seeds of communism in the political parties of France, and—since doubtless he was responsible for some of the notorious acts of terrorism in the thirties—also may be considered the father of anarchism.

Buonarroti, however, remained throughout these later years very much the power behind the Republicans. After 1830 he was the party's Dalai Lama, whom the initiated, including George Sand, alluded to in vague terms and whom no one ever saw. It was Heine again who warned against "this terrible enemy of the existing order, who lives in the subsoil of society." He predicted that Buonarroti's teachings would have formidable consequences.

In 1835 the party's official front was still held by Armand Carrel, who kept the program within constitutional lines. Republicanism, at least on the surface, looked much less dangerous than it actually was or sounded in the mouths of some of its members. The radicals, however, pressed toward a more active public propaganda. They found a suitable occasion in the great April trial.

This trial, sometimes called the Republican monster-lawsuit, involved twenty-two leading members of the Republican party and more than eighty workmen and members of secret political societies. All were accused of fomenting strikes in the industrial centers, strikes which at times assumed the proportions of civil war.

The trial took place in Paris before the Court of Peers. Of the hundred and sixty-four members of the court, only two-thirds showed up. More than a hundred liberals of every color had flocked to Paris to give support. But in the end only accredited lawyers were admitted to the defense, among them Michel de Bourges, Dupont, and Armand Carrel. With the stage set for enormous publicity these men intended to make the trial a huge demonstration in favor of their party politics.

The trial lasted, in all, nine months. The opportunities for propaganda were ample but came to nothing, owing to the dissension and lack of diplomacy on the part of lawyers and defendants alike.

The prisoners made the initial mistake of going on strike after the first session of the court. They wrote a joint letter accusing the court of partiality and duress, insisting that even the pretense of justice was lacking. They declared that thereafter they would remain in their cells rather than appear before such a court. The measure of course availed them nothing, as the chamber went into session without them.

The next blunder was committed by the lawyers, who also decided to write a letter of protest and to have it published in the *Tribune* and the *Réforme*, both liberal papers. The missive was another diatribe against the Peers and ended in the defiant phrase: "The infamy of the judge is the glory of the prisoner!" The letter was signed by all members of the defense counsel.

The Peers immediately conducted an inquiry into this business and discovered that two-thirds of the signatures had been falsified. They pinned the letter on Michel de Bourges and the physician Trélat, a Republican and former Carbonaro, and put them on trial too. Trélat was given a large fine and three years in prison. Michel got off with one month in confinement.

The political defendants, numbering more than a hundred, were sentenced to deportation or to five, ten, or twenty years of detention. Fortunately, before the trial was over, a number of the prisoners had managed to escape by digging a subterranean corridor in the best Monte Cristo fashion.

The public was rather relieved when the trial was over. Parisian burghers had at first delighted in the perpetual commotion of the day, and had celebrated the Republican cause with nightly illuminations and promenades on the crowded boulevards. Then they had tired of the spectacle and in the end, like the conservatives, were glad that it was over. The rebels were beaten and could cause no more damage. Business needed a legal, not a revolutionary government, and Louis-Philippe had emerged from all the confusion quite triumphant. They approved of his measures

against the associations of workmen and political reformers, and settled back contentedly to the daily tasks and joys
which promised to run smoothly from then on.

The Republican party was dissolved, its leaders in prison
or in hiding. But Michel de Bourges was made famous by
his thirty days in jail. A hero and a saint, George called
him. Their friendship took on a deeper and more passionate hue.

George had known Michel in the glorious days of the
July Revolution of 1830, when he had headed the Republican list of Berry deputies, and George and her husband had
personally canvassed votes for him. He was then a liberal
lawyer of local repute only. But by 1835 he had become a
political personality of nation-wide prominence. His radicalism, backed by enthusiasm and a legal mind, made him
a great asset to the party.

George had gone to see him in Bourges shortly before
the trial started. Two of her Berry friends, Planet and
Fleury, went with her. Perhaps she desired some information as to the forthcoming trial in Paris; perhaps she needed
his friendship for more personal ends. She asked him for
advice concerning her possible separation from Casimir, but
Michel advised against it for the time being.

His personality seemed disappointing. He made her think
of Engelwald the Bald, title hero of an old Tirolese song,
who in lonely altitude chased the chamois. Yes, he was Engelwald—Everard, as she will call him a little later. Life's
battlescars had marked his limbs and face, he was old and
bent. George, with a recently acquired knowledge of phre-
nology as taught by Lavater, began to scrutinize his face at
once. Nose, chin, and brow betrayed tremendous energy,
the curve of his nostrils fine intelligence. More admirable

still was the dome-like skull that showed the evenly bal-
anced superiority of his mind. He was a great man after all.

Michel, too, was impressed. George's dark, passionate
eyes obviously pleaded for his recognition of her as a woman,
though her words implied only a desire for information and
instruction. All night, with Planet and Fleury, they walked
the dark deserted streets of Bourges. While the moon rose
and set again beyond the dark outline of the medieval cathe-
dral, Michel gave an exhaustive and fervent description of
the tenets and aims of the Republican party.

"My friends," he admonished George and her companions, who listened half skeptical, half overawed, "ours is
the great task of completing the Revolution of '89. The torch
of Babeuf and Robespierre is flaming in our hands and we
must pass it on—now! Their great ideal, the sovereignty of
the masses, must finally be realized.

"Much blood has been shed in defense of this doctrine,
but truly I tell you: more catastrophes are to come. We must
be ready for the ultimate sacrifice while serving this one
great idea. Castles will be leveled to the ground, rivers will
be red with the blood of the fighters—yes, our whole generation may perish in this last struggle. But what does it
matter if the idea remains victorious, if a new era will rise
from the ruins—an era of happiness, harmony, and liberty
for all?"

"And what will happen in the meantime?" interrupted
the cynical Fleury. "Have you a workable party program?"

"There is one program only," said Michel, scowling.
"Robespierre's declaration of the Rights of Man, equal rights
for all! Secret ballot, universal suffrage, freedom of the commune, freedom of the press, the right to organize, free and
progressive education, reorganization of state credits, liberation of the workman from the yoke of capitalism through

an equal distribution of work and the instruments of labor, introduction of trade unions, European federation, free trade, and equal rights for all European nations."

"Good God!" Planet exclaimed. "That will lead us straight into anarchy. The people are not ripe for such innovations. They cannot yet rule themselves!"

"That's why we need a strong central government, chosen by vote, which will regulate production and protect the equal rights of every man. Believe me, my friends, this battle for the liberty and dignity of man is a great and noble one. Personal sorrows pale before the impact of such great and universal aims and problems. But we need much love to solve and realize them—consummate love placed, in the name of our Creator, at the service of all mankind. Not the individual, but universal human welfare, deserves our full devotion."

George and her friends left the following morning as unexpectedly as they had come. It was Fleury, the soberest among them, who hurried them away. Michel's Republic had given him nightmares.

Yet the spark that was to kindle the friendship between George and "the great man" already was alive. George soon published the sixth of the *Letters of a Traveler*—to "Everard" instead of Musset.

During the April trial George and Michel de Bourges were both in Paris, and Michel was a daily guest at the Quai Malaquais apartment. With him came a whole phalanx of Republican colleagues, many of whom had an official connection with the great lawsuit. George's small apartment now rang with the violent verbiage of the excited patriots. The sweeter, more sentimental vocabulary of the poets, which included "soul," "love," "passion," and "beauty," gave way to "freedom," "equality," and "sov-

ereignty of the people." To most of George's guests the
overthrow of the government seemed imminent. God only
knew but what tomorrow this or that obscure lawyer or
politician now smoking in a corner of George's room might
be a minister. They were all busy distributing the different
portfolios, each one thinking first of himself. Michel's famous letter to the Peers, published with the falsified signatures in the *Tribune* and the *Réforme*, may not have been
written at the Quai Malaquais, yet, according to Marie
d'Agoult, George was present when it was drawn up.

George's new political enthusiasms left her somewhat
neglectful of her artist friends. Occasionally she saw them
in the afternoon, at the trivial tea hour. The evenings and
the moonlit nights belonged to the Republic. Michel would
appear at six p.m. and take her out to dinner, where over
onion soup and fried chicken he would tell her of the rhe-
torical laurels he had won in court that day. If the weather
was pleasant, they would go for a boat-ride on the Seine,
though it did not quite live up to the beauties of the Grand
Canal. Nor were the moon and the stars quite so bright
here as over the Venetian lagoons. After a while they would
descend from their "gondola" and take a few steps on the
boulevards filled with excited crowds venting their political
passions in jokes, laughter, and clever repartee until the early
morning hours.

The more deeply George became interested in the mysteries of Republican politics, the more intimate grew the
relationship between master and pupil. Hastily the over-
turned altar of Eros was re-erected, the sacrificial basins
re-adorned with roses.

But the new love was tame and timid compared to the
torrents of earlier days! George's soul seemed to have lost
its unlimited urge. She loved in Michel the idea rather than

the man himself; nor was the idea altogether a satisfactory one.

At times, when this modern Robespierre was talking to her, propounding his doctrines of world catastrophes, the pupil hardly listened. Michel, suspicious of her acquiescent silence, would shout at her: "You let me talk but you do not listen! You receive my words, phrases, metaphors like a melody or a poem, but you are not convinced by them!"

And George would say inwardly: "No, I am not convinced when he rides his hobby. He is sick and hysterical when he talks himself into a policy of destruction. Why, those old-fashioned ideas of Babeuf and Buonarroti mean nothing to us any more! Division of the soil? If you like. Reduction of private property to a minimum? If need be. But no private capital, no inherited property at all? Impossible! It would run counter to all the inherited instincts of mankind."

Yet at the same time she would write a letter to her son Maurice, then a student at the Lycée Henri IV. "Among the men who defend property at the point of the bayonet [this in connection with the reactionary spirit in the National Guard] there are more fools than villains. In most cases it is the result of an anti-liberal education. . . . Tell me if you feel it is just to divide the products of the earth so unequally among men——the fruits, the grain, the flocks and herds, materials of all kinds, and above all gold! Tell me whether the division of property is equitable when one man has an enormous share, another much less, a third almost nothing, and a fourth nothing at all." The twelve-year-old boy is further admonished not to pay too much attention to his professor's dissertations. "Their books are dictated by pedants who are slaves of some power."

Yet George's ultraradicalism was not very sincere. She had the instinctive conservatism of the mother of a family, and objected to the uncompromising political and social demands of her friend Michel. She demanded protection of the family, protection of a minimum property, protection, most of all, of the human personality, whose free development must be safeguarded. Michel's theories seemed to her inhuman and anti-social. What right had he to impose his destructive and false truths on her mind?

"As a woman and an artist I must hold a different point of view," she told him angrily.

"Quite right, Madame," Michel would answer. "You taught me some time ago that your soul has a sex. It is feminine, Madame! And that has been quite a disappointment to me. From your book *Lélia* and your *Letters* I had derived the impression that it was masculine. I saw you as a poet, not a poetess. I expected this poet to be my pupil and my son, who would inherit my ideas and continue my work. Well, it seems I was wrong! My pupil is arrogant, unjust, and stupid : he knows nothing and does not want to learn anything, or only at high speed. Quick, quick, God's secrets for Monsieur George Sand, for he cannot wait. That is the way you approach the absolute truth."

George would laugh at this; her irritation never lasted long. But she loved Michel best when he was tired and had his "face of sixty years," for then he was "gentle, simple, sincere, and filled with divine aspirations."

Did she love him? Her literary output during these years offers a curious mixture of what was on her mind. There is *Simon*, the novel in which she fully proclaims her Republican ideas. Not that the plot differed much from the former ones, but its hero, Simon, is no longer the Romantic

filled with vague melancholy at the senselessness of all occupation, but an ambitious professional with a brilliant
career ahead of him. Also "he had sucked Republican ideas
at his mother's breast. His father, an old veteran of the first
Republic, had been killed by the Chouans."

Simon's antecedents show a distinct similarity to Michel's,
while the heroine Fiamma might be likened to George, at
least in her efforts toward social justice. Fiamma tries to
level class differences by seating the modest peasant woman,
Mother Féline, next to the proud wife of the subprefect,
and she actively furthers Carbonarism—the revolutionary
doctrine imported from Italy. When she first meets Simon
she hails him with the battle-cry of the true Carbonaro:
"*Evviva la libertà!*" and then discourses with him on Italy's
freedom.

There is also a "Letter to Everard," filled with generous
praise for true Roman Republican qualities: temperance,
charity, constancy, diligence, and unselfishness. But if Everard preaches virtue, she—George Sand—will preach honesty, because while virtue is not necessary for everyone,
honesty is. For honesty means "instinctive wisdom, natural
moderation, and the absence of turbulence, or rather of
those stormy passions which prove so disastrous to society."
Yes, she will forever praise honesty above all other qualities, though she herself is still far from virtue or honesty,
temperance or even morality.

Side by side with such stern literature she produced a
series of novels written in a lighter vein, such as *Mattea*,
L'Orco, and *L'Uscoque*, dealing with incidents and anec-
dotes from Venetian history. Though of no great importance, these novels have grace and seem written easily, as if
springing from some mysterious longing for Venetian
nights, lagoons, music, beggars, and historic monuments.

In the fall of 1835 George, with Michel as her official counselor, started suit for legal separation from her husband. Her marriage had become impossible. Casimir during one of their many disputes had threatened to throw her bodily out of the house. The trouble began over a pitcher of cream, but back of it were incurable irritation and dislike. In February the Civil Court of La Châtre rendered a judgment in favor of Madame Sand.

George, who had spent a winter of most circumspect behavior at the house of her La Châtre friends, returned joyfully to Nohant and took possession of her house. She dismissed the servants, keeping only the old gardener and his wife. To get rid of the last traces of Casimir's former presence she changed the furniture around until the rooms looked again as they had in her grandmother's time.

The triumph did not last long. Casimir appealed to a higher court, and the suit was brought before the Royal Court of Bourges, Michel's home town. This time Madame Sand's books as well as her whole private life stood trial. All her early adventures were discussed, including her chaste romance with Aurélien de Sèze, whose love letters were read in court. The newspapers, according to their liberal or conservative policies, took sides for or against her.

In the midst of the battle Michel remained cool and superior. He knew how to distribute the psychological lights and shadows and with Machiavellian subtlety managed to paint Casimir as the dissolute, brutal, barbarous peasant husband who had for years tortured and terrorized a noble genius.

Swept by Michel's eloquence, the prosecutor himself took sides with George's cause. But the judges were a tougher crowd. They hesitated to set up a precedent favoring all-too-willful wives. Finally the litigants settled out of court.

George took some Paris real estate which Casimir had acquired, in exchange for fifty thousand francs in cash. She also had the guardianship of the children. The father had the right to supervise the son's education, and to have the children visit him once a year. George, in a letter to her half-sister Caroline, complained of his pettiness. "He not only wants to see the children, he expects me to pay for their trip. Tender loving parent! When we settled our belongings he did not shrink from demanding through his lawyer fifteen pots of marmalade and an old iron stove valued at one franc fifty."

With the jam-pots finally settled, George could shelve her matrimonial experience, though Casimir made one futile effort to kidnap his daughter Solange—an attempt nipped in the bud by the energetic interference of her mother. Thereafter their relationship remained peaceful and friendly. Casimir married his housekeeper and acquired a new family.

The children on their part were willing to submit to their mother's lone leadership. They even adopted her pen-name and thereafter called themselves Maurice and Solange Sand. The matriarchy was complete. And to do George justice, she incurred no loss whatsoever—financial, moral, or artistic—when she let Monsieur Casimir Dudevant slip into obscurity.

CHAPTER TWO

Liszt and the Irrational

THE elopement of Franz Liszt with the Countess d'Agoult, wife of a high member of the French aristocracy, had considerably shocked Paris society. But the couple had retired quietly to Geneva, and the fires of moral indignation had died down from sheer lack of fuel. No one knew that Marie d'Agoult had borne a daughter to Liszt. The child, Blandine, was boarded out immediately after her birth. Liszt could give concerts and attract a large circle of new pupils without the Calvinistic citizens of Geneva objecting or throwing stones.

George Sand had been, in a way, the lovers' patron saint. They had read *Leone Leoni* together; over it they had wept and fallen in love.

Then Liszt had conducted Madame d'Agoult to George's apartment on the Quai Malaquais and there—as George told it—Marie had seated herself between the two poor artists, George and Franz, like a heavenly apparition. George felt like a peasant girl or an unkempt student in Marie's presence. With her jewels, her expensive clothes, her haughty manner, this woman might have roused her antagonism had not George continually reminded herself that the countess dared to put into practice Madame Sand's most revolutionary theories about personal freedom and emancipation. Marie had left husband, children, money, and a high social position to live in free communion with the man of her choice.

George, after accepting Marie as a friend, gave her all the devotion and admiration of which she was capable. But more than Marie, she admired and respected Liszt. George's friendship for Liszt had, however, all the signs of an *amitié amoureuse*. Marie d'Agoult, who had had her misgivings about it, wrote in her diary at a later date: "I have realized how childish I was to think—and the thought was painful indeed—that George and George alone could have brought Franz's artistic potentialities to the fore, and that I was nothing but an unfortunate barrier between two destinies ordained to penetrate and supplement each other."

Liszt was twenty-five years old. He was the world's foremost pianist, his musical compositions brought him money and fame, and society loved and spoiled him for his genius as well as for his handsomeness. His brow, resembling Dante's, was luminous; like Faust he yearned for God and transcendental knowledge.

None of George's earlier friends had been quite like Liszt, not even Sainte-Beuve with his *air de soutane* and his delight in whispered secrets. None had been able to give advice on metaphysical truth. They all could deal with aesthetic and moral facts but were out of their depth in the transcendental world.

Not so Liszt. George saw him as "the exceptional being,

FRANZ LISZT
After a lithograph by Kriehuber

the precious vase into which heaven has poured its special gifts."

Once their friendship had been firmly established, Liszt urged George away from the politicians and demagogues and turned her toward the great spiritual advisers of mankind, to the leaders of official and unofficial creeds. He opened up vistas of which she had been but dimly conscious before.

George renewed contact with the Saint-Simonists because the spiritual and emotional implications of their creed appeared in another light when interpreted by Liszt. She attended their meetings regularly from now until 1838. She was introduced to the teachings and ritual of the secret lodges, and became interested in the mystical plottings of Ballanche, who was reviving spiritualism, and the sect of the Illuminati of Lyon. The mystic wave emanating from Liszt also carried her toward Lavater, admirable friend of all living creatures, who believed in progressive divinization of man and had a kind word of defense for even the worst display of human weakness. "Had I known Lavater," George told Liszt, "he would have had unlimited power over me. For this mighty mind, combining so much virtue with so much wisdom, influences me even from the grave."

Having read Lavater, she could introduce into her "Letter to Liszt" the following mystical paragraph, leading the reader into a demon-inhabited world: "Nature was probably not created exclusively for man, or else before he came to rule the earth numerous rural divinities existed, who have not yet completely retired into their heavenly sphere, their scattered groups still living on in deserted places. This explains the awe we feel when treading virgin ground, the alternating fear and joy we experience in lonely places.

Why should the echo of our steps make us tremble in abandoned cloisters? What makes so strange the trackless beach, the unclaimed prairie, the empty house? Do we not feel the presence of the invisible beings whose realm it is, and who have the right to welcome or to oust us?"

Lavater's great contemporary, Goethe, had expressed himself similarly, but in a shorter and more poetical way:

> *"Heil den unbekannten*
> *Höhern Wesen die wir ahnen!*
> *Ihnen gleiche der Mensch.*
> *Sein Beispiel lehr' uns jene glauben."*

(Hail to the unknown superior beings whose existence we surmise. May man emulate them and in so doing teach us to believe in them.)

George's momentary spiritualism was a last faint echo of the theosophical beliefs of 1770. The Romantics, though thrilled by the idea of ghosts (the supernatural is colorful), would not be converted to so much unscientific nonsense. But they eagerly accepted Lavater's other great mystical theory: that all art is divine inspiration. His words: "Whoever is not a prophet is not a poet; all true poetry is an inspiration of the divine mind!" found a happy response in their hearts.

George considered Lavater's occultism a preparatory step toward the loftier and more comprehensive spirituality of her own contemporary, the Abbé de Lamennais, whose disciple she was shortly to become. The magic power of the living is stronger than that of the dead, and the benevolent face of the Reverend Lavater paled before the energetic profile of the solitary genius of La Chênaie. Lamennais believed in Christ and not in ghosts, waived demoniac in favor

of divine inspiration, and traded a vague humanitarianism
for active socialistic propaganda. Liszt had for years been
dominated by the man and his ideas; he was eager that
George too should come under his influence, feeling that
her art as well as her humanity would benefit.

Once more George's soul was ready for surrender. She
met in Lamennais a frail, narrow-shouldered priest with
ascetic features, a prominent nose, and obstinate forehead.
He gave her the hard unsympathetic stare of a true mis-
ogynist, for the strong-willed priest, like Saint Paul, considered women essentially his inferior. Yet he did not scorn
George's proffered collaboration. She, as well as her friend
Madame d'Agoult, might prove effective carriers of his
ideas. Also, they might support his private charities. In spite
of their many objectionable adventures and their circle of
gossip-laden literati they seemed harmless enough and
might be allowed to run along with his other importunate
followers. He allowed Liszt to bring the two women to La
Chênaie, and eventually he was seen at their Paris salon.
But his visits were few, and at one of George's receptions
he happened to meet Heinrich Heine, who drove him away.
Not that Heine had been aggressive or impolite, but the two
men were diametrically opposed in character and point of
view. Heine had involved Lamennais in an argument on
Christian socialism. He had been sarcastic, and Lamennais
had lost his self-assurance when faced by his opponent's
brilliant dialectics. "The man has something satanic," he
wrote afterward in his diary. To the priest Lamennais,
Heine represented the most demoniac of all symbols—
doubt.

Yet Lamennais was one of the great French liberals of
the day. Originally an orthodox Catholic priest, he had almost become a cardinal but had suddenly revolted against

Rome and decided that liberalism and Catholicism must join forces. The Pope was to be the spiritual leader of the new popular movement, charged to regulate and purify it. Together with Lacordaire, Gerbet, and Montalembert, all ardent Catholics, Lamennais founded *L'Avenir*, a liberal magazine advocating separation of Church and state, no government funds for the religious cults, liberty of association, free lay instruction, and the universal ballot. But the leading French clergy, Legitimist and Gallican in its attitude, refused to follow, and Pope Gregory XVI, who was bound up with the Metternichs of Europe, was even less inclined to heed the danger signal. Without mentioning Lamennais by name, he condemned him and the magazine in his encyclical, *Mirari vos*, with the result that Lamennais turned definitely away from the Church and espoused the radical cause. He published *Les Paroles d'un Croyant*, in which he demanded full recognition of Christ's dogma, but otherwise sided with the democratic ideals of '93. No one was to be master, no one servant; military service was to be abolished, and also the autonomy of the Church; all private property must be reduced to a minimum. In some of his points he foreshadowed the Christian socialism of Pope Leo XIII, in others the evangelical idealism of Tolstoy. He based his teachings exclusively on the Gospel, insisting that it contained all a Christian had to know.

Lamennais's political demands were less important to Liszt and George than his theories on art. *L'art pour l'art* is nonsense! Art is divine revelation. For only God, who inspired the New Testament, had the right to call things by their names. All human language is remembered, not invented. These conclusions, which he took from the dogma of the Traditionalists, emphasized Lavater's demand that the poet be a prophet and vice versa. But Lamennais had amplified this statement. Art is revelation, and derives its contents from the contemporary, ruling ideas, or rather from the faith, knowledge, and scientific perception of a given historical epoch. Each epoch is permeated with ideas which are specifically its own. These ideas are of course only relatively true, as each epoch is limited by its own potentialities. But art must serve this truth, even though it is only relative: it must express the noblest and purest tendencies of the day.

Liszt had compressed these ideas into *Génie Oblige!* Following Lamennais's lead he had written a series of articles proclaiming that art had no other aim than to manifest human progress. He maintained the necessity of musical instruction for the masses, and considered his own artistic career to be an educative and social mission. Thus in 1837 he gave a concert for the Lyon strikers.

Nor was he the only one to take up Lamennais's theories and give art its social due. Saint-Simon had already taught that the artist was divinely inspired and destined to be the educational leader of mankind. The great Victor Hugo had also expressed his full faith in the artist's role as prophet and priest. But neither of these men had convinced George. It took a man like Lamennais, a deep believer, a faultless, pure, and sincere Christian with the halo of a martyr, as well as a friend of the people, to win her over to the formula. Michel's advice that she direct her energies toward impersonal ends and values found an ideal and comprehensive elucidation through Lamennais's teachings. At last the road into the immensity of heaven was opening up. The artist as prophet, as demonstrator of divine truth? What a career! George recognized her final mission within society: to be a leader and a teacher through her work. With renewed eagerness she bent over the well of inspiration, trying to find in the reflection the higher meaning given it by God Himself.

The influx of all these ideas for which Liszt was responsible may be likened to the injection of another, mightier dose of Romanticism. George's new spiritual convictions found expression in her novel *Mauprat*, which she wrote while the judges debated on her divorce.

Mauprat, possibly George's best novel, was published in the *Revue des Deux Mondes*. It is the story of a family of feudal seigneurs and cut-throats of Berry who had survived into the nineteenth century, holding peasants in serfdom. They never read books, but loved to quote Charlemagne, Louis XI, and Louis XIV in support of their feudal prerogatives. If they caught an innocent wayfarer on their roads they held him for ransom, or even cut the tendons of his feet. Bernard, last of the Mauprats, would have embarked on a similar career of lawlessness had he not fallen in love with his cousin Edmée. Under her superior influence he turned from a brutal, dissipated beast into an enlightened, moral being. The feudal theories of predestination were overcome. The spiritual man triumphed over the sensual one.

Her new convictions were carried over in her "Letters to Marcie," which she published in Lamennais's magazine *Le Monde* chiefly to help the dying paper. No longer did she demand the complete emancipation of women, as she had in *Indiana*. "Women complain of their state of slavery. . . . Let them wait until man has first freed himself . . . something else is more important for the moment, the permanence of a morally improved plane of living. . . . Whatever harnesses the instincts, fortifies the will, and leads human emotions into regulated channels helps establish God's kingdom on earth, which is nothing else than the supremacy of love and truth on earth!"

Several of the "Letters to Marcie" had been published in *Le Monde* before Lamennais happened to read them himself. He was much shocked that such frivolous and minor matters were being discussed in his high-toned paper, and forbade further publication of the letters. The pieces ceased to appear and there was a temporary strain in the relations of George and her Christian philosopher. But she, with her customary kindness, took the blame on herself.

She had gone to Nohant to recover from the worries of her divorce; in the midst of the peace and beauty of the Berry landscape, and the affection of her children and her many friends—perhaps in the face of altogether too many highly moral resolutions—the urge for variety and life came to the fore again. She suddenly longed for Liszt, the faraway friend who had been responsible for her many new inspirations. She wrote to him and Marie in Geneva: "Life is a desert. . . . You, my two friends, are the noble palms in whose shadow I shall rest and gather new strength."

She left Nohant for Switzerland in September 1836, accompanied by her two children and a nursemaid, joining the Liszts in Geneva. and in their company went to Chamonix.

CHAPTER THREE

Romantic Friendship

THE tourists at Chamonix had their sensation that fall in a group of mysterious strangers in slouch hats, tight-fitting coats, and enormous ties who were stopping at the Hôtel de l'Union. It was hard to determine their social level, harder still to determine their sex, for the men seemed dressed as women and the women as men. Occasionally two young girls, obviously of good family, were seen with them, and a beautiful blond woman whose dignified behavior showed that she, too, belonged to the upper classes. Yet it was impossible to find out who was master and who was servant, or how many men or women were in the party.

The hotel proprietor had reason to be annoyed, for their registration cards had been filled out in the most misleading manner. On one was written:

Name of traveler	*the Piffoël family*
Residence	*Nature*
Where from	*from God*
Going to	*Heaven*

Place of birth	*Europe*
Validity of passport	*Eternity*
Issued by	*Public opinion*

A second card proclaimed the Fellowe family, whose head called himself a musical philosopher, born on Parnassus and traveling from Doubt to Truth.

The Fellowes and the Piffoëls, or the Liszt and Sand families, had been joined by two friends: Pictet, a gaunt, sober-looking Swiss major, and Hermann Cohen, alias Puzzi, who was Liszt's favorite pupil. Puzzi liked to hide his long boyish limbs in girl's clothes, and as George and her daughter Solange wore boots, trousers, and blouses most of the time, changing to women's clothes only on formal occasions, much of the spectator's confusion was caused by these three.

One thing was sure: they were having a delightful time. They played jokes on each other and fell into each other's arms; they philosophized continually; even on mule-trips up the most dangerous mountain trails they would speculate whether the Absolute were identical with itself. Liszt asked the questions which the major, their encyclopedia, would answer in a precise and academic way. The countess astonished them all by the glamour she lent even to her platitudes.

George was the only one who did not enter into the spirit of these conversations. She liked to interrupt with a joke, mainly because the major annoyed her; he was condescending and questioned her intelligence! She protested against the superabundance of logic. "I don't care for your German philosophy," she countered. "It dries up the heart, frays the nerves, and corrupts the divine mysteries within us, never allowing for a generous mood or a religious or human emotion."

The major pitied her for her inadequate intellect. She had irritated him from the first. When, in Geneva, he had asked her how she liked Switzerland, she had told him that everything in it was banal, and that nature would be banal too if it had a chance.

She gave him nightmares. One night he saw her as a huge black cat spitting fire, jumping on his bed and tearing his books and papers to shreds. But in the morning he felt more lenient toward her, especially when she had one of her imaginative moments and amused the party with her tales. Thus she had one day discovered the "British effluvium." "The inhabitants of Albion," she told them with mock dignity, "are surrounded by a special effluvium which makes them waterproof on their long travels. It is owing to this effluvium—not their three pairs of breeches, worn one over another—that they arrive clean and dry in the worst rain and mud. Because of it their hair never flies, they appear freshly shaved and manicured on all occasions. It covers them like a thick-walled diving-bell and in the center of it these British eat, sleep, drink, promenade, and travel around the world. None of their curls is ever out of place; their shoes and gloves never develop holes. One might say, it is not they who travel, but their wardrobe. And their diaries ought to show the following entries: Walk of a hat in the Pontine marshes—Memoirs of a cape in Switzerland —Trip of a raincoat around the world."

"Bravo, George!" Liszt applauded heartily. "You are a great scientist. Long live the British effluvium!"

But the countess had a queer look on her face. George was evidently aiming at Marie's own English way of dressing. She smiled with difficulty. "What a charming notion, my dear George. How clever of you to divert us from our dry philosophy by your amusing tales." Turning to the major, she added: "I find George's gaiety quite contagious, although no one would say that happiness is a frequent guest on my brow."

The major nodded eagerly, not without an adoring glance at the noble and suffering brow.

George tickled the back of Liszt's mule with a thistle until the mount began to kick and the musician almost lost his balance.

"George is a child," said the countess emphatically. "Always up to some trick." That night she noted in her diary: "George's silly jokes annoy me . . . as a consequence I am not very amiable . . . which saddens me, as I am eager for her friendship. But the more depressed I become, the more I lack in kindness."

Before returning to Geneva, Liszt called on Moser in Fribourg in order to test his famous organ. It became a memorable occasion for all. Never had there been such a performance of Mozart's *Dies Irae* in the church of Saint Nicholas. Liszt's magic touch evoked all the organ's sonorous beauty.

"Quantus tremor est futurus."

George, remembering the text of the hymn, felt excited, and a flame of new vitality swept over her. She watched Marie d'Agoult leaning against one of the columns, motionless and untouched, her beautiful profile turned toward the light.

Their journey had proved, on the whole, a happy experiment, and the Liszts and Sands decided to continue living together. "Princess Arabella," as George called Marie, wanted to recover the role in Paris society which she had abandoned with her elopement. She had always enjoyed being the brilliant center of a group of clever and prominent people. But it was possible that society might snub her now. She needed moral support, perhaps an ambassador of peace. She turned to George for help.

The Paris salon of the Countess d'Agoult and Madame Sand was outwardly a modest one: a small impersonal living-room in the Hôtel de France, without any special charm. But Liszt introduced his musician friends and George attracted the political and literary element. Among the more frequent callers were Sainte-Beuve, Lamennais, Leroux, the Polish poet Mickiewicz, and Heine. Of the women who came, perhaps the most brilliant and original was the Princess Belgiojoso. But the most indispensable was the wife of the Spanish consul—talkative, busy, officious, enthusiastic Madame Marliani. She estranged friends, reconciled enemies, mediated, arranged, procured, paid bills, lent, borrowed, and was all in all the best and most devoted friend George and Marie possessed. French women kept aloof—Paris society continued to ostracize the novelist and the woman who loved Liszt.

Nevertheless their drawing-room was the most brilliant of the season. The *esprit* of the guests proved almost too much for George, who was seldom brilliant in society. She tired quickly of too much conversation, and her heavy consumption of cigarettes was proof of her boredom. Like Lamartine she insisted that genius needs fresh air and is corrupted by the cleverness of the salon. She missed Nohant. At night she wept because she could not see the sky and hear the wind in the linden trees. After two and a half months of social life in Paris she left suddenly for Berry. Marie followed a month later, because she could not or would not keep up her social activities alone. More likely she wanted to escape from her love, for Franz had become the source of much grief to her. Sick in body and soul, she joined George in Nohant.

George too had her troubles. Her friendship with Michel de Bourges was in its final phase. "Robespierre" grew daily more morose and indifferent, and was somewhat belatedly discovering his conscience as a father and a husband. Vainly George urged him in her best literary manner: "Appear, my lover, and, invigorated like the earth by the first rays of the sun in May, I shall shed my shroud and tremble with love. The signs of suffering will disappear from my brow and I shall be young and beautiful, for my body will tremble with joy in your embrace of steel. Come, come, and I shall be strong, sane, young, happy, and full of hope."

But Michel stayed at home, or yielded but rarely to her entreaties. There would be a hurried rendezvous half-way between Bourges and Nohant. George would come storming down on the black mare which she had trained to do "a hundred miles a second. . . . Sky and earth disappear when she carries me along under the blossoming apple trees."

When she returned at dawn the mood was over. There was relief at seeing her own four walls. "Hail, Piffoël, full of grace! Wisdom is with thee. Blessed art thou amongst fools. The fruit of thy suffering hath matured. Holy fatigue, mother of sleep, descend upon us poor dreamers . . . now and in the hour of our death. Amen."

Women are apt to grow confidential under the stress of their love-troubles. George and Marie had never been so intimate before. "I like it here very much," Marie reported to her friend Ronchaud. "My affection for George is growing. The country suits her better than Paris."

Both kept careful diaries, and the things they noted down during these weeks were surprisingly similar. They watched the boatmen pull their towboats up the River Indre. The meadows were filled with forget-me-nots, daisies, and red thistles. Sometimes a family of geese crossed their path.

Cows carried their rocking shadows across the pastures. Summer and the smell of new-mown hay were in the air.

George lay in the grass and described the microscopic world around her : "My sense of proportion was lost and the charming grasses, swaying in the breeze, seemed like beautiful trees shaken by a frightful storm. Here was a slender pine, there a weeping willow with its head bent low. A bit of quaking grass showered its gigantic fruits on my hair, and a few feet hence a deep forest jungle opened up before me."

When she felt warm on her walks or rides she threw herself fully dressed into the river, letting the sun and air dry her afterward. In company with the countess she hunted butterflies and rare insects—Goethe had set this fashion, and the countryside offered ample opportunity to follow it. At any rate, peasants, horses, dogs, fields, and woods seemed much more important now than all the literature in the world.

The countess had, as usual, attracted a train of admirers. Every male between twenty and sixty within a range of many miles was at her feet: Bocage the actor, George's childhood friend Didier, Mallefille, the private tutor of Maurice, and many others. George, far from being jealous, took part in the general worship. She admired Marie's beautiful hair, impeccably curled even out here "in the rough" (Marie had a special maid to do her hair in the morning) ; she admired the thin creaseless veils, admired the costly clothes, admired the whole precious "Princess."

Liszt still saw in Marie his goddess. He came to Nohant in June, contributing his own poetic note. His presence made Nohant much more attractive to both women. "Ah, if someone could love me that way!" George exclaimed with envy. When she awoke in the morning and heard the first measures of the *Pastoral Symphony*, her own depression gave way like mist before the rising sun.

George's Journal for June 12 reads: "Tonight while Franz was playing fantastic melodies by Schubert the Princess walked in the shadows that fell across the terrace. Her head and slender tall body were swathed in a long thin white veil. I watched her move back and forth with a light tread which scarcely touched the ground—the circle she described was cut across by rays from my lamp, around which all the moths of the garden were dancing a delirious saraband. The moon behind the lindens threw into high relief black specters of pine trees that stood immobile in the blue-gray air. . . . We others were seated on the steps listening to the strains of the *Erlkönig*. As the prelude gave place to the heartbreaking refrain we sank into the mood of surrounding nature and were engulfed in melancholy enjoyment. And we could not take our fascinated gaze from the magic circle traced before our eyes by the mute sibyl in white. When the music merged into tender melody her steps grew slower.

"From that time onward her pace kept the rhythm of the andante and the maestoso, and her movements showed such marvelous harmony that it was as if music flowed from her as from a living lyre."

The shadow of the countess continued to recede and approach. Her rhythm and the melody were one, "until the lovely phantom came to rest on one of the pliant lilac bushes. Then, as if it had been bound by some mysterious ties to the pale beautiful woman, the music stopped."

This synchronization of two spheres of movement with a third near the spectator's lamp is a piece of magic never accomplished by George's contemporaries. Not until Marcel Proust's *Swann's Way* has such rhythmical fusing of threefold action been described with the same ease and the same power of observation. It requires an intensely musical temperament.

Liszt always paid homage to George's musical sense. The musical tradition in her family derived from the famous Mademoiselle de Verrières, who had staged musical comedies at her house and had been a well-known singer. Marie-Aurore de Saxe, George's grandmother, had inherited these talents, and studied Porpora, Hasse, Pergolesi, and Gluck, accompanying herself on the piano. Her son had been an accomplished violinist, and George herself had studied the piano. But as her husband had hated all music and fled at the sound of her piano, she had given it up. Later her nostalgia for music was poured into her two most brilliant novels, *Consuelo*, and *The Countess of Rudolstadt*.

For the moment she was happy to have the foremost contemporary pianist at her home. She said of Liszt's music: "I love the broken phrases which he flings from the piano, and which rest with one foot in the air, dancing off into space like little lame elves. The leaves of the lindens steal the melody and complete it with mysterious whispering, as if they were confiding nature's secret to one another."

Liszt's musical interpretation intensified George's and Marie's emotional response to nature. He tried always to express nature through his music, for like all Romantics he believed in an underlying relationship between them. Often the three discussed the problem, and in favor of their arguments quoted the German Romantic writer, E. T. A. Hoffmann (or his famous character, Kapellmeister Kreisler).

"The sound from the north—the sound from the south." These key-words from a posthumous work of Hoffmann caused long-lasting arguments in Madame Sand's salon. Some of the questions could be answered only by George, the poet.

Marie d'Agoult wrote in her diary: "This morning George spoke to me about the differences between the sounds from the north and from the south, and between the sounds of nature in winter and in summer. She said a very simple thing, which, however, has never been said before. She said that the summer wind dying in the leaves has not the sharp whistling sound of the wind hitting dry branches. And water flowing through dense forests and green meadows has a different murmur from water rushing between bare river banks. She said the observation could be generalized and enlarged. One would then find in nature a basis for music. This observation was of course not that of a scientist. Only a dreamer and poet in love with nature could muse and listen long enough to come to such conclusions. And he has to be a musician besides.

"I do not know how true this is. I don't know whether man may be allowed to penetrate the mysteries of creation and discover the laws of sound, color, and smell."

Liszt and George were profoundly stimulated by Hoffmann's fantastic theories of the identity of color, sound, and smell. Kreisler's poetic ramblings seemed expressly written for them: "Yes, often when I lay in the grass, leaning against the stone and listening to the wind whispering in the tree-tops, it would sound like sweet celestial voices, but the melodies I heard had long lived within my breast and had simply come to life now. . . . I saw inside the stone. Its red veins opened like dark carnations whose fragrance rose visibly in high singing rays. The long resounding notes of the nightingale changed their rays into the shape of a beautiful woman, but the form would then dissolve again into heavenly wonderful music."

Some of George's guests smiled at these queer ideas, calling them artificial or fanciful. But George met their opposition with the remark that even the noblest human language was still too barbarous to translate adequately these intuitive glimpses of a higher world. "These things are so true—indeed, so obvious—that even the artist cannot fully express them. Hoffmann with his broader and more precise vocabulary was simply able to make us understand one of the most exquisite of all musical and visionary experiences." She added that Hoffmann's foremost characteristic must have been "the power to wonder."

Fruitful were the summer days, doubly fruitful for the fancies and emotional sensibilities of George and Liszt. But slowly and naturally as a season changes, the friendship drew to an end in coolness and separation. In July Franz and Marie left Nohant for Italy. The letters they exchanged with George were filled with vows of friendship, but the terms of endearment were already tinged with criticism and dislike. Each contended that the other had not written; both were reluctant to write. Then too George had other sorrows. Her mother died, and though Sophie Dupin had brought only trouble and disaster into her daughter's early life, George was greatly affected by her death.

Occasionally the name of her son's tutor, Mallefille, appears in her letters. He had consoled George for Michel de Bourges's departure, and in the eyes of her friends Mallefille had seemed ill-mannered and much too ambitious. They had been shocked by the affair. Marie d'Agoult was the first to complain about the rough young man. George had reconciled her at the time with a pleasant word. She herself did not think Mallefille's faults so serious, but a little later she commissioned her philosopher friend, Pierre Leroux, to dismiss the importunate lover. Now Chopin had crossed her path, and George was on the point of proposing to him by means of a long explicit letter to his best friend, Grzymala. Chopin had belonged to Marie d'Agoult's court of admirers, and his shift to George's camp was possibly a cause of the dissension between the two women. But the true cause of their enmity must be sought at the beginning and not at the end of their friendship. Rocheblave, one of George's best-informed French biographers, gives this summary: "Their souls were even more dissimilar than their faces. Once they saw each other without prejudice, they could not see each other at all."

The discord between them was emphasized by their differing social points of view. George was the democrat, a friend of the people and a believer in social equality. Marie was the aristocrat, always conscious of the prerogatives of her class. Even during the periods of their greatest intimacy they were not really friends. Marie said in her memoirs: "She never surrendered herself. I never really had her confidence." And she gave the sum total of their relationship on the first page of her novel, *Julien*, which contained the following dedication to George:

"We wanted to be friends!"

CHAPTER FOUR

"The Angel with the Face of a Grieving Woman"

LISZT said of Chopin: "The total impression was one of harmony. His gaze seemed spirited rather than dreamy; his sweet and noble smile knew no bitterness. His delicate, transparent skin was a delight to the observer, his blond hair was like silk, his nose slightly hooked; his movements were distinguished and his behavior so aristocratic that everyone treated him as a prince. His gestures had grace, the tone of his voice was low, often choked; his figure was not tall, his limbs looked fragile. Those who came in contact with him were struck by the harmony of his appearance, work, and performance. Legouvé, a friend of Berlioz, used to call him a delightful trinity: his gaze resembled the tone he drew from the piano, the utter delicacy of his skin could be likened to the poetical sadness of his nocturnes, and the exquisite care with which he dressed seemed to explain the worldly elegance of some of his work."

Chopin met George in the fall of 1836, but refused to pay homage to the two bluestockings at the Hôtel de France.

He was a prude, full of prejudices. He had known Marie in the days of her social glory, and her adventure with Liszt had not increased her value in his eyes. Concerning George, he had made only one comment: "What an utterly unsympathetic woman!"

Apart from Heine, Liszt, and a few Polish friends he associated exclusively with the nobility of the Faubourg Saint-Germain. They adored him, paid highly for his music lessons, and subscribed to his private concerts, which were famous for "their audiences of princes, ambassadors, duchesses, and cabinet-ministers." He was not robust but his health gave no cause for anxiety. He considered himself engaged to Marie Wodzinska, the daughter of a Polish count.

Chopin, being the son of a modest Warsaw school-teacher and never having known a brilliant home, must have enjoyed like a long happy dream these years of glamour and success. He became fastidious in his tastes and liked to spend his money on expensive clothes, luxurious furniture, and elegant dinner parties. He loved flowers. His aristocratic friends, the Countess Delphine Potocka, the Princess de Beauvau, the Princess Czartoryska, never arrived without bringing roses or orchids, which he would arrange in a costly vase. He worked on his compositions and was happy.

But the dream had a rude awakening. Pressed by her parents, Marie Wodzinska broke her engagement to him. Her family may have been influenced by class prejudice, but they also feared—and with certain justifications—that their prospective son-in-law was consumptive.

Chopin's biographers usually deal lightly with his first love-sorrow, but it became important enough to prevent his facing life normally and sanely again. Not even George's strong maternal hands could lead him out of this *impuissance de vivre*. It was now that melancholy marked his traits; George spoke of him as "the angel with the face of a grieving woman."

After the break with Marie, Chopin lived through a period of utter despair. He could not commit himself, could not find relief in talking about his grief. Shyness and reserve made it impossible for him to confide even in his best friend. He took refuge in solitude and hypochondria.

Paris, however, was not the city to leave a famous young man to his melancholy. One night when Chopin was alone as usual, with his rooms in darkness and only the grand piano lighted by a few candles, Liszt broke in noisily, followed by a crowd of prominent people: Heine, Meyerbeer, the tenor Adolphe Nourrit, Hiller, Delacroix, Mickiewicz, George Sand, and Marie d'Agoult.

Chopin gave them a polite welcome, and after a while seemed ready to share in their fun. When sufficiently stimulated he could be witty, high-spirited, and—as George called it—full of intellectual coquettishness. He was famous for his impersonations, could bring the most absurd characters to life with the aid of a cap or shawl, and was particularly successful in the presentation of "traveling Englishmen, spinsters, and mothers-in-law." George had already loved that sort of thing in Musset.

That night, after having contributed to the general entertainment by his play-acting, Chopin grew serious. He sat down at the piano and improvised. George listened to him from the depth of an armchair and was "strangely attentive and full of sweet acquiescence."

From that night on, George and Chopin saw more of each other. In a little while George wrote to Madame Marliani: "I cannot answer your letter fully now because, as you know, the weather is variable in the mating season. There

FREDERIC CHOPIN
After a painting by Ary Scheffer

is a great deal of—yes, no, rather, but. Sometimes we say in the morning: 'This is intolerable,' and at night: 'It is ultimate joy!' I am waiting until my emotional barometer is more stable before I let you know what is happening."

If George had made her plans concerning Chopin, they were maturing now. Chopin was willing to submit to her strong personality with its strange charm and maternal solicitude. He was attracted also by the comforts of her home. Years before, when he first came to Paris, an unknown music student living in an attic, a woman from the floor below had invited him to her quarters. The pure young man refused to go, but noted regretfully in his diary: "I would have found a fireplace and a fire, and I could have warmed myself." Eight years later, with George offering him the protection and warmth of her house, he hesitated no longer. He accepted—though not without a last gesture of resistance. But eight years of homeless life had wearied him and made him ready for concessions.

George had suspected some of his scruples. In a confidential letter to his friend Grzymala she deprecated his exaggerated sense of propriety: "He [Chopin] seemed always to cry 'shame' over man's lowness, the way old women do, and he blushed at the memory of earlier temptations as if he feared to soil our love, should he let himself go. To judge men and women's ultimate embrace in this manner has always been odious to me. If this embrace is not as holy and sincere as everything else, let not those who wish to be abstemious call their attitude 'virtue.' I dislike the phrase 'physical love,' which designates something God alone has a right to name. Can there be purely spiritual love for one who is sincere with himself? Can there ever be love without a single kiss, and kisses without voluptuousness? To be con-

temptuous of the flesh is well for those who have sensual
thoughts. But if one loves and still insists on chastity, let
him do so out of respect rather than contempt."

Earlier in this famous letter, which so thoroughly sums
up her attitude toward love, George had implied that her
relationship with Chopin was no longer platonic. She speaks
of a heavenly storm which had for moments carried them
away to other regions.

"Nevertheless we shall have to come down to earth," she
continues to tell Grzymala, "even if we have been divinely
aroused and have journeyed across Elysian fields. Poor birds
that we are, we have wings but we nest on the ground, and
when the song of angels bids us heavenward, the cries of
our family bring us back to earth again. I do not want to
abandon myself to my passionate impulses, though they may
still lurk in the recesses of my heart. The thought of my
children will give me strength to avoid all other entangle-
ments, and in a manner most propitious to their health, education, and happiness. Thus I cannot move to Paris on
account of Maurice's illness, etc., etc. Also there is in my
life an excellent being, perfect as to heart and soul, whom
I will never abandon. He has been with me for a year now
and is the only person who never once, not for a minute,
has made me suffer by his own fault. He is also the only
man who has given himself completely to me, without regret for the past or concern for the future. But he is so kind
and wise that I can make him understand everything; he is
the malleable wax on which I have set my seal, the imprint
of which I can change at any time if I use caution and patience. But today this cannot be, and his happiness is sacred
to me. . . .

"My duty is therefore clear. But without repudiating it,
I can live up to it in two different ways. One is to keep away

from C [Chopin] as much as possible, not try to enter into his thoughts, never find myself alone with him. The other way is to get as near to him as possible, without compromising the safety of M [Mallefille], to remind him of me in his relaxed and happy moments, to take him chastely in my arms when that heavenly storm threatens to carry us away into the skies. I will adopt the former way if you tell me that the woman in his life [Marie Wodzinska?] will give him real happiness, will take care of him and bring love and harmony into his life, and if under the circumstances my presence would be a disturbance. His soul, from an excess of foolish scruples, may perhaps refuse to love two different beings in two different ways, and may think that the eight days spent with me once in a season could interfere with his domestic happiness. Well, then, if that should be the case, I shall make him forget me."

In the following paragraphs George brings up the question of Chopin's marriage, and comes to the conclusion that it is not advisable for him to be married—to another woman. She rather visualizes a union between him and herself, but along these lines:

"Personally I would arrange our 'poem' in such a way that I would know nothing of his positive life and he would know nothing of mine; he would follow his religious, artistic, social, and poetic inclinations without my making him account for them, and vice versa; but whenever and wherever we met, our souls should be at their climax of goodness and happiness. . . .

"As far as the question of possession or non-possession is concerned, it seems to me of secondary importance. Nevertheless it is important enough in itself, it is a woman's life, her most cherished secret, her profoundest theory, her most mysterious *coquetterie*. Let me confess to you, my brother and my friend, what my secret is—though others have commented on it before, and in strange manner indeed. I really have neither theory, nor doctrine, nor fixed opinion, nor prejudice, nor pretension to great virility, nor any silly spiritual notions in this direction. I have no preconceived ideas, no habits, and I believe no false principles, either of license or restraint. I have always trusted my instincts, which were always noble. I have sometimes been deceived by others, never by myself. I have committed many follies, but no mean or trivial deeds. I have heard many comments on human morality, modesty, and social virtue, but I do not see clearly in this and have as yet drawn no conclusions. . . . My emotions were always stronger than my reason, and the limits I tried to impose on myself proved useless. I have changed my mind twenty times. I have believed in fidelity. I have preached, practiced, and exacted fidelity; people have failed me and I have failed them. Yet I cannot repent, because my infidelity has always been mixed with a sense of fatality—with an instinct for the ideal which made me abandon the imperfect for something nearer to the perfect. I have known several kinds of love: artist's love, woman's love, sisterly love, motherly love, a nun's love, and a poet's love. God knows what other loves! Some were born and died the same day, without their object ever knowing anything about them. Some of my loves have tortured my life and brought me to the brink of despair, nay, insanity. Others have held me in a purely spiritual bondage for years. . . . Those who saw but the surface of things called me mad and hypocritical, but those who read in my heart know that I loved beauty and truth, had a sensitive soul, a weak judgment, an absurd, trusting character which was never petty or vindictive; that soul knew no scorn or ire, and quickly forgot the evil in things and men."

Whatever overcame Chopin's virtuous resistance—George's casuistry, her passionate will, or the pale flame of Chopin's own sensuality—George won him over to her viewpoint in the end. Chopin was twenty-seven, and George thirty-three. Chopin was a sick man; George wrapped him in the protective warmth of her maternal love—and she was still a beautiful woman. Balzac, who dropped in at Nohant at about this time, found Comrade George in yellow slippers and red trousers, with a cigar in her mouth, and wrote to his friend Madame Hanska: "George has the double chin of an abbess, but not a single white hair. Her clay-colored skin is unchanged, her beautiful eyes have their luster of old. . . . She has been in Nohant a year now, a strong, sad woman who works enormously." He added: "After all, she is a man and wants to be a man, and has given up her role as a woman. A woman attracts and she repels, and as I am extremely male myself I think other men must react to her as I do. Her man is hard to find."

For once she had been silent concerning her conquest. No longer would she broadcast to the world that she was in love. This new happiness of hers was to remain cloudless and hushed, like a beautiful summer Sunday. Perhaps she was discreet for the sake of "that poor Mallefille," whose pride and feelings were probably deeply hurt.

Then she wrote to her publisher: "Money, Buloz. I need more money!" Again she was ready to carry her love into a distant land. Chopin also prepared for a prolonged absence. He sold his *Préludes* (as yet unwritten) to his publisher Pleyel for two thousand francs, and took five hundred on account.

The two lovers had decided to go to Mallorca, and told their more intimate friends that Maurice's rheumatism necessitated a trip south. Chopin, in need of a rest, was simply accompanying the family as a friend, almost an older son. George no longer needed to complain, as in the days when Musset had departed from Venice: "Whom shall I nurse now that you are gone?" She had her hands full, and realized it. She called Chopin her *"cher cadavre."*

They reached Palma de Mallorca in November 1837 in glorious weather, but an unpleasant surprise was in store for them. Palma had no hotel, not even an inn. There were no furnished rooms, and the French consul had difficulties in finding them shelter. Finally, outside of Palma, they discovered a small villa with a beautiful location but no furniture.

The tropical colors, the abundance of fruit and flowers, delighted them. Small houses built in Arabian style were pleasantly exotic, and Chopin wrote joyfully to Paris: "It is hot; at night there is singing and the sound of guitars . . . a marvelous life!"

After three weeks the rains began, and the green hills, the flowers, and exotic little houses became indistinguishable under a mist of gray. Their house had no stoves— only open braziers which filled the rooms with suffocating fumes. The dampness was so pervasive that the plaster fell in flakes from the ceiling and food mildewed in the cupboards. The wind hurled itself against the house, shook the lemon and myrrh trees in the garden, and whipped the rain against the windowpanes. The lovely trails changed to deep gutters where turbulent waters carried mud and stones downhill.

Chopin was much affected by the weather. He began to cough, caught laryngitis, and had to stay in bed. The landlord, hearing consumption mentioned, gave notice and added a huge claim for damages on the grounds that Chopin's sickness had made the house unfit to be lived in. George furiously upbraided the natives for superstitious idiots. But pay and leave she must. As they could not possibly sail for France in this weather they looked around for another house. But the Mallorcans refused to take them in.

Three miles outside Palma, far up on a mountainside, was the monastery of Valdemosa, mostly in ruins but with a few cells intact. In summer the city rented them to tourists, but in winter they were empty. George could do nothing but move in and make the best of it. In the eyes of the natives they were lepers, destined for isolation.

The rooms contained a few camp-beds, straw chairs, and a sofa with no upholstery other than a few cushions stuffed with sheep-wool. Clothes were kept in the family trunks. A large white shawl served as curtain for the alcove and the floors were covered with straw mats from Valencia, or snow-white sheep-skins. A huge native vase adorned their only iron stove, which a Palma blacksmith had made especially for George.

Chopin felt forlorn and wretched. There he was, half-way between mountains and sea, his clothes ungroomed, his hair untidy, and his face pale—more pale than ever. The storm came howling down the mountain, shrieked in the gables and wailed through the corridors. A waterfall roared in the distance, and far, far away, the sea surged with unabated fury against the foot of the hill.

To Chopin the house seemed a cemetery, his room a mortuary vault. Cypresses grew in front of his windows. He had hallucinations, heard the singing of the long-departed brethren and felt their ghostly breath on his cheek. The food was nauseating to him, the wine made him sick. The bread on the table was moldy, and the milk drawn from their despondent little goat did not suit his taste. He grew so irritable that a fly on the wall threw him into a rage.

But the letters sent off to Paris betrayed none of their discomfort. George did not want her friends to say, as in the days when she had gone to Italy with Musset: "Ha, they thought they would have a good time and now they have the cholera."

"Don't tell anybody that I have been sick," Chopin warned Fontana. And George declared: "The idea of ever leaving the peace and calm of Valdemosa frightens me."

Fortunately for Chopin his grand piano arrived. The shipping had been costly and complicated but now the noble instrument was by his side. His sufferings almost forgotten, he gave himself up to the wealth of melodies surging from unknown depths within him. Besides the *Préludes* promised to Pleyel, he composed two *Polonaises*, his *Scherzo No. 3*, a mazurka in E-flat, and his second *Ballade*. Even his life at Valdemosa found a faint echo in his work: some of his happier moods—sunshine, a child's laughter— and then again the monotony of falling raindrops and the wind wailing between empty walls.

George had finished her novel *Spiridion*, which she had begun in Paris under the guidance of her friend Leroux. She also revised the second volume of *Lélia*, and decided that her "cloister scenes would have been ever so much better and more original if I had written them in Valdemosa." But in her interpretation she was far from sympathetic to monasticism. "How can a modern person desire to live a life of such God-like exclusiveness? Maybe it suited the medieval monk who wished to serve God and his ascetic ideals far from the barbarous strife of his time. But we no longer have the right to live that way. Seclusion of an individual or a few privileged groups cannot be tolerated in an age which knows a different sense of solidarity and puts man under obligation to serve modern progress in common with his fellow-man."

Spiridion was her first anti-clerical novel, and its spiritual father was Lamennais, although Leroux may have been responsible for its ideas of "solidarity" and the "transmigration of souls." But the Abbot Spiridion is Lamennais himself, with his doubts, hopes, sufferings, and his fateful evolution from a strict belief in monotheism to a broader understanding of the Divinity. Spiridion's final creed represented something like Christian socialism. The principles of liberty and equality it contained were drawn from the Gospel of Saint John. He welcomed the French Revolution in the name of the "sans-culotte" Christ, and believed it was destined to establish God's kingdom on earth.

Buloz thought the story too mystical but published it nevertheless, and because it was timely, like her other work, it was a success. It touched on a subject of high popular interest: Lamennais's struggle against a crude and materialistic clergy and the reactionary papal court. Rome's prestige-politics was considered a grave danger to European democracy, and the liberal element had supported Lamennais's claims and accusations to the full.

Naturally George could not remain silent on such an important issue—she remembered too well the spirit of her Voltairian grandmother, whose attitude toward the Church had been summed up in the words: "One meets these things with decency and respect, but does not believe in them." George went beyond the attitude of outward acquiescence and secret dissent. She had to fight in the open; the cause of human progress deserved her militant support. *Spiridion* was her first attempt in this direction.

With the end of the rainy season, they left Mallorca. After a last painful interlude on the boat, where they were held in quarantine with a shipment of pigs, they landed thankfully in Marseille. They decided not to move north until Chopin's convalescence was complete. When they finally returned to Nohant it was May, and they had been gone almost nine months. George must have blessed the sight of Nohant's walls, if only for the sake of her finances; possibly she remembered another earlier return—from Spain, the day she had come to Nohant with her father, mother, and blind brother. A strange old lady with a blond wig and rouged cheeks had stood in the doorway and taken her into her arms with a gentle smile.

George was through with traveling. "I am no longer a bachelor, and you cannot travel with a family." George found herself tied down to home life and stability once more.

CHAPTER FIVE

Preparing 1848

"FATE impelled us into the bondage of a long association; we got into it without quite knowing why."

Chopin had followed George to Nohant for two reasons: he needed her care, and he was too conventional to treat their relationship as a passing adventure. George reasoned that Chopin's tender affection would protect her against other, more reckless affairs which were no longer appropriate to her social position and her role as mother of adolescent children. She had no passionate feelings about Chopin. Habit kept them together. George called it "fate."

In the fall of the same year they left Nohant for Paris, because life was cheaper there than at home, where a continuous stream of visitors allowed no economies. They rented two small one-story houses in a quiet courtyard off the Rue Pigalle. Chopin had one of the cottages for himself, but he took his meals with George's family and received his friends in her salon.

In the course of the winter George met all of Chopin's

Polish friends. Her favorite was Mickiewicz, the poet and mystic, whom she considered more important than Goethe and tried to popularize among the French reading public.

Chopin had to adapt himself to the mixed circle of Madame Sand's friends. He was not a democrat; the dirty boots of the proletarian poets and the crude manners of George's Berry friends got on his nerves. Among her philosopher friends only Lamennais appealed to him, and among the artists he tolerated Heine and Delacroix. He liked the singer, Pauline Garcia, Malibran's younger sister, whom George adored for her talents and her kindness. He even courted her a little, but on the whole he preferred his own friends, the Rothschilds, Baron Stockhausen, Countess Potocka, and the aristocracy among the Polish refugees, with Prince Adam Czartoryski and Princess Anna Czartoryska heading the list.

Laube, Gutzkow, Balzac, and others have put the interior of 16 Rue Pigalle on record for future generations: the small coffee-colored antechamber, the green salon with its flowers, Chinese vases, Chopin's piano of palisander wood, paintings by Delacroix and Calamatta—last but not least, George's chestnut-colored bedroom with brown rugs, brown velvet chairs, wall-coverings of brown rep, and the Turkish divan which served as her bed.

Already George's home had become a museum, a place on exhibition for tourists, foreign and otherwise. If George had had a sense of irony she would have smiled occasionally, remembering the attic she shared with Sandeau, or the dilapidated *palazzo* where her doilies had adorned Pagello's armchair.

Perhaps she would ask her mirror once in a while whether this museum life were not aging her prematurely. But her friends could reassure her on that score. Edouard Grenier, a

young man who saw her then for the first time, recorded in
his memoirs: "In some ways she was more beautiful than
I expected her to be, in others she was less so. She had been
famous when I was still in school, and that seemed very
long ago. Yet she was only thirty-six years old now. Short
and stocky, very simply dressed in a black dress with high
collar, it was her head that commanded attention, and her
head by the eyes. Her eyes were wonderful—though too
closely set—large, with long black lashes, but without luster, like unpolished marble or rather like velvet, which made
her gaze obtuse and cold. . . . Her high forehead, the black
hair parted in the middle, the beautiful quiet eyes with
their finely shaped eyebrows, gave her face an expression
of strength and nobility which the lower part of the face
did not share. Her nose was fleshy, without contours . . .
her mouth lacked in finesse, there was a rather conspicuous
double chin. . . . As for the rest she was utterly simple in
her conversation, her attitude, and her gestures."

Others have written of her voice. Heine mentioned it in
Lutèce: "Her voice was faint and veiled, without sonorous-
ness but sweet and agreeable." Her biographer Caro spoke
of its "cold, lazy tones."

Whatever the general impression she gave, her contemporaries crowded her salon, wandering, startled and filled
with curiosity, among the few intimates. George was bored
by them. She smoked incessantly, throwing the stubs into
small water-filled trays standing on every piece of furniture. She spoke very little, and what she said sounded trite.
Occasionally her native temper broke through—her "Rabe-
laisian vein," as Madame Ollivier had called it. This highly
conventional Swiss lady had eyed George critically through
her lorgnette and decided that the famous Madame Sand
was a woman rather than a lady. In her presence a lusty

"bitch" had escaped from George's mouth when a young woman had entered the room with too spectacular a rustle of silk petticoats.

Most of the time George kept in the background, gentle but mute. She was no longer Lélia making a demoniac and tempestuous entry wherever she went. She no longer wore red roses in her black hair. Like a good responsible homemaker she worried about health, work, and family finances. The passionate pulse had slowed down, the terrific hunger for knowledge seemed stilled. Was it age? But the forties were still far away. Chopin? He could never be the focal point in her life. Essentially nothing bound them together except George's maternal care. But each lived within the cell of his own artistic individuality, and nothing, no spark, could bridge the void between them. Chopin would never share in any of George's worries—his nerves did not permit it. Indeed, the smaller the event, the greater was the turmoil. "Chopin's emotions have no relation in size to their cause," George noted time and again.

No, Chopin was not responsible for whatever peace of mind she had acquired, nor was Lamennais or Sainte-Beuve, but a small man in a shabby coat, whose boots scratched the inlaid floors of her salon, who moved awkwardly and stuttered and burdened everyone with his money troubles and family affairs. Yet he caused George to exclaim: "He has saved me! His books gave me peace and solved all my problems!" He was Pierre Leroux.

Thanks to Leroux, Lélia had found the restorative at last which promised her wisdom and truth and a frictionless transition into an age of sober reflection. She wrote to her friend Marliani: "God's kindness is great that He allows us to grow old and quiet and to suffer no more from the stings of individuality which made our youth so bitter. Why do we complain, when there is so much to gain in the end—larger and better ideas and a conscience which may reconsider the past triumphantly and exclaim: my task is accomplished! The hour of fulfillment is near."

But at this moment Chopin, the children, and a few intimate friends were with her at Nohant. It was May again and the rainless days called for walks and long excursions. George and her friends went on foot; Chopin rode a circumspect little donkey. At night the guests played billiards in the great salon; there were charades and pantomimes.

Delacroix had come down from Paris, to the great joy of Chopin, who loved him tenderly. Both were utterly fastidious as to their clothes and loved to discuss their tailors and the latest exigencies of male fashion. Also Delacroix adored and understood Chopin the musician and never tired of listening to his playing. Chopin, though respecting Delacroix the man, detested Delacroix the painter. As George said, "Chopin accepts Delacroix's adoration and is touched by it, but when he looks at his friend's canvases he suffers and cannot say a word in their praise. He is a musician and nothing else. . . . He understands nothing of painting or sculpture. Michelangelo frightens him. Rubens horrifies him. Everything eccentric scandalizes him. He desires the most conventional and narrow. Strange anomaly—for he is the most original and individual of all artists. . . . And as a matter of fact, Delacroix's literary tastes too are of the most classical and formal kind."

Though they differed in their points of view the two men often entered into long discussions about art. Delacroix never tired of drawing analogies between painting and music. He said: "Harmony in painting is established by the relationship of colors—even by the grouping of their reflections. The same holds true of music. Its harmony is brought about not by the construction of chords, but by their interrelationship, their sequence, their effects—by what might be called their auditive reflections, the reflection of a reflection!"

Chopin went to the piano, struck a few tentative chords, and sighed. "I find nothing at all—not color, not even a design. I find only shadows and their reflections, vague outlines——"

"Ah, but you have not finished yet," Delacroix objected. "Try to find the design and you will find the color."

Chopin patiently tried again, found *la note bleue*—the key he needed—and finally lost himself in a melody of his own—in the words of Proust: "those long-necked, sinuous, and measureless phrases which come from somewhere far away to strike finally into the very heart of things."

That night George recorded the scene in her diary, ending with the words: "His hands find the 'blue sound' which carries us far away into the transparent night. Clouds dissolve and reshape into fantastic designs, spread across the sky, press after the moon which throws large opalescent disks at them and brings back the color which had gone to sleep. We dream into the summer night; we wait for the nightingale!"

CHAPTER SIX

The Children's Crusade

THE years 1840–48 were a long step toward the Revolution, for George as well as for the rest of France.

Yet the surface of things was prosperous and there was even something like a boom. Guizot's phrase *"Enrichissez-vous"* had seized the middle class like a fever. Their desire to get rich quickly was furthered by fruitful speculations, first in cane- and beet-sugar, then in railroad shares. Though Thiers had had no confidence in the future of the steam-driven engine and Arago had predicted that transportation of soldiers in railroad cars would make them effeminate, the first two French railroad lines were successes. The government, after having bought the property and constructed the lines, turned the management over to the bankers for speculation. The values of shares boomed instantly. People hastened to subscribe to the latest issue. Bankers were as busy as in the days of the fantastic Mr. Law, and Rothschild was the hero of the day. Thureau-Dangin, the conservative author of the *History of the July Monarchy*, reported that, thanks to the country's inner and outer peace, wages and the price of real estate doubled, government bonds increased steadily in value, and the workmen were better dressed and fed than ever before. The farm laborer acquired the habit of wearing shoes and stockings, and the working-classes ate white bread and meat, and drank wine with their meals.

Factional strife began to subside. Rossi wrote in the *Revue des Deux Mondes* in 1842: "The public is interested only in business and speculation. It has no taste for politics; it rather fears it, for it does not want to be disturbed. But each epoch seems to have its particular enthusiasms: the Empire had the bulletins of the Grand Army; the Restoration had liberty and the Charte; now we have wealth! People with a generous disposition ought to do well these days."

People began to distrust the parliamentarism which had proved a source of corruption under Guizot. They called the parliamentary regime a worn-out machinery. Young deputies entering the Chamber in 1846 prided themselves on their anti-parliamentarism and spoke of the illusions of their liberal forerunners.

The Romantics, too, had lost their glamour, though George Sand, Sandeau, and Chateaubriand were still best-sellers. But the ruling passion for money had invaded even literature. Possibilities of making easy money in this field arose when Emile de Girardin popularized the press. Girardin, a brilliant young journalist with anti-radical tendencies, created a new type of journalism. In place of the old journal which cost eighty francs a year, had a restricted circulation and a definite policy, he founded a journal which cost half the price, was larger in size, catered to a non-political reading public, and went in for stock-exchange reports and advertising. Girardin fought a duel over this question with the Republican Carrel, owner of the *National*, and killed him.

A main feature of the new journal was the *roman-feuilleton*—the serial story. It made a success of the whole enterprise. Dumas and Balzac were under contract to newspapers for huge sums. Eugène Sue, the most popular fiction writer of the day, was paid 100,000 francs for his *Wandering Jew*. Appearing in the *Constitutionnel*, it raised the circulation from 3000 to 25,000 readers. The story was the talk of the town, its characters and incidents were discussed at every breakfast table, and it was reported that Marshal Soult became furious and turned the war ministry inside out when one of the installments was missing. Thureau-Dangin remarked reproachfully that the bourgeoisie amused itself with this literary dirt, and that the proletarians of the Paris suburbs, who also read it, were more than ever convinced of the rottenness of the upper classes. But Sue was very popular with the poor. One desperate young fellow hanged himself in Sue's apartment, leaving a letter saying: "I kill myself in despair, but it is easier to die under the roof of one who loves and defends us."

Sue, George Sand, and the poet Béranger were considered the chief interpreters of the woes of the masses. And woes there were in spite of the new prosperity, which meant profit to the financial aristocracy only. The new speculative trend in business and commerce made for greater tension and insecurity. It also depleted the state treasury. Exhaustive armaments in 1840, when France almost went to war with Turkey over the Mehemet Ali issue, and later the building of railroads, had necessitated continual loans on the part of the government. This gave the bankers an ever-recurring chance to plunder the treasury and that part of the public which invested in state bonds.

Reform seemed necessary. If the rich disdained the new reform movements and social Utopias, those who had less money and more *esprit* championed them eagerly. They were backed by the Republicans, who had resumed their activities since 1840. The party had meanwhile split into a left and a right wing. The right wing or political Republicans wanted mainly political reforms; their organ of publicity was the *National.* The left wing or socialist Republicans went in for economic revolution; their official paper was the *Réforme,* directed by Louis Blanc and Ledru-Rollin. Both parties pulled together when the government had to be opposed, but were bitterly divided on matters of revolutionary policy. Nevertheless, the ideas of political liberalism waned before the onslaught of the socialist doctrinaries. Industrial liberalism had filled the moneybags of only a few, and parliamentarism had culminated in nothing better than the corrupt dealings of Monsieur Guizot and his retinue of ministers and bankers.

George was as usual a barometer indicating the change in opinion. She treated the current problems in *Horace.* The year before she had published her *A Winter in Mallorca,* and two rather insignificant love stories. But *Horace* marked a new departure. It was the first of her so-called socialist novels.

Horace, and with him other young men in the story, already embraced the ideals of the new decade. They no longer held the point of view of the despairing young Romantic of 1835 who exclaimed: "When shall we be free? When shall we be taught that modern man is like Anthony, Manfred, and Didier, and carries his own law within his bosom?" The young radicals in *Horace* want freedom for others rather than for themselves; they speak of justice and solidarity. They praise man in the mass, the anonymous proletarian, and despise the egotism of the liberal-minded bourgeois. France, they feel, can be saved only by its proletariat, who will lead the country eventually toward an artistic, social, and political renascence.

Buloz refused to take the manuscript; there was a limit to what he could offer the patient readers of his middle-class review. George had to publish *Horace* in the *Revue Indépendante*, which had recently been founded by Leroux and Louis Viardot, Pauline Garcia's husband and director of the Opéra-Comique. The review was ill-managed and almost caused George's financial ruin, but it supplied her friend Leroux with a living and helped him support his nine children and several unemployed brothers. And George gladly made the personal sacrifice, because Leroux was the one person necessary to her spiritual wellbeing. She loved him because he was simple and kind. She needed him because his philosophy gave her the answers she sought.

Compared to Lamennais, Leroux was mediocre and painfully shabby. He was a printer by trade—half proletarian, half bourgeois, with neither education, culture, manners, nor even outward cleanliness. His gestures were as crude as his words, and strangers made him so shy that he stuttered when he had to answer their questions. Yet he had a name as journalist as well as philosopher. He had conducted the *Globe* with Victor Hugo, Chateaubriand, Béranger, and Guizot as his collaborators, and he had proselytized the Saint-Simonists even before the July Revolution. Buloz had at one time published his articles and criticisms in his *Revue des Deux Mondes*, but had given it up when Leroux began to write about God. "God is not timely!" Buloz had told the startled little philosopher.

His contemporaries called him vague and second-rate, but modern critics have dealt more kindly with him. Faguet called him "a great mind whom no one ever took the trouble to explore." George thought him genuine enough to serve her own purpose. His philosophy appealed to her heart as well as to her mind because, as someone judiciously said, "it was sufficiently obscure to keep going the enthusiasm of people who live by their emotions rather than by their reflections." She found that his philosophy contained the thought of all her favorite reformers, from Rousseau to Lamennais. Leroux had systematized their more important ideas into a doctrine of his own, the basis of which was human solidarity. He had borrowed the term from the current political dictionary. We cannot live outside human society; our passions, senses, and reasoning powers are by no means individual; we share them with the whole of humanity. Within us lives the spirit of the ages, and from century to century life feeds on what life has created.

Since we owe knowledge and feeling to humanity, we must use them for humanity's good. Humanity is the ideal, which we represent individually—and it is dependent upon our good will, so we must make the effort to realize the ideal. In conformity with Plato, we must gravitate toward God, the ultimate beauty and perfection, in unison with others, changing the world by living up to the principles of organization and subordinating our individual will to the great and universal law of solidarity.

George, after having adopted Leroux's philosophy, turned it into fiction. Her novel, *Consuelo*, which appeared in 1842–43, was a literary sensation. Never before had she so astounded the public by the virtuosity of her inventive genius. The canvas on which she depicted her story was spacious enough. Through the singer Consuelo we are introduced to the brilliant eighteenth-century stage of Venice and Vienna, to the splendor of absolutist royalty. But George, with her love for the humble and hidden, finds no satisfaction in depicting the bright surface only. She uncovers the sores of feudal oppression; her sympathies go to the poor and disinherited, particularly to the small and sorely tried Czech people, unwilling subjects of the Austrian crown. And here she applies Leroux's dogma. She goes after the deeply hidden symbols of the nation, not as expressed in art but rather in the artless—in its folksongs, its national tunes, and finally in its eternal struggle for liberty. What so many biographers have derisively called her "musical" mysticism found utterance in many true and beautiful statements, particularly in regard to national music: "Speaking of the power to awaken emotions and to present things in an entirely new and original aspect—certain anthems will evoke the gigantic phantoms of ancient cathedrals! . . . Those who are able to express simply and powerfully the music of different nations, and know how to listen to it, need not, in order to behold different nations, make a tour of the world, visit their monuments or read their books, traverse their mountains, their plains, their gardens, their wildernesses."

Surely those sentences could not have been written without the inspiration of Chopin, the musical nationalist par excellence. But without Leroux she would not have been able to formulate these things. With him she came to the conclusion that the arts of a nation as well as its struggle for freedom and higher spirituality were but the outward manifestations of its progress toward God.

The Countess of Rudolstadt resumes the plot where *Consuelo* leaves off. But the center of interest is shifted from music and Consuelo to the dealings of the secret societies which played so important a role in the history of the revolutionary movements up to the middle of the nineteenth century. The "Invisibles," a secret international order that tests Consuelo's political loyalties, have all the characteristics of revolutionary plotters.

"We have two modes of action," explains the head of the hooded court. "The one, material, is to undermine and destroy the ancient world by criticism, by examination, by raillery and Voltairism. . . . Our other mode of action is entirely spiritual, and devotes itself to founding the religion of the future. The elite of the intellectuals and the virtuous assist us in the unceasing labor of our thought."

George obtained the data of the secret societies from Leroux, who probably held a membership in one of the contemporary occult sects. Because of George's great interest in Masonic matters he may even have introduced her to that society, for much of the material in *The Countess of Rudolstadt* links up with Masonic ritual and tradition.

George's other great novels of the 40's, *The Journeyman-Joiner* and *The Sin of Monsieur Antoine*, belong to a different series. Less mystical and sublime in their ideas, they were more up-to-date in characters and plot. Their heroes, young workmen and artisans, usually married young and enlightened countesses and went through life advocating socialist theories. Whatever capitalist entered the plot was doomed to perdition, or at least rebuked for his wrong philosophy.

Exaggerated as the plots and situations may seem, George gave an essentially true picture of what was happening in the country. She registered what she saw and knew, and what contemporary history had to offer. And her socialism was effective with people who would never have listened to an actual representative of the working-classes.

They listened to Madame Sand because she was famous. Doumic, one of her best French biographers, said that her theories made an appeal to intellectual snobs, with the result that much conservatism was undermined and much solid prejudice shattered to bits.

For her most daring novel, *The Sin of Monsieur Antoine*, she at first found no publisher. Not even the liberal papers would take it, their circulation being too limited to allow for Madame Sand's prices. Curiously enough the *Epoque* took the story. George said of this paper that it topped all others in reactionary and absolutist policies, and yet gave her the freedom to express her radical ideas to the full in its columns. Also it gave her publicity. Huge red and yellow posters shouted from the walls along the Paris streets: "Read the *Epoque!* Read *The Sin of Monsieur Antoine!*"

The book presents the story of the slow industrialization of a small rural district. The head of this district, the industrialist Cardonnet, surprisingly has all the virtues of an honest, well-meaning citizen. He is capable, industrious, and free from cant. Of his many sensible phrases Emerson copied at least this one: "Beware of preaching. It is but the expression of self-satisfied vanity."

Cardonnet considers himself the savior of the impoverished village of Gargilesse and the countryside around. And rightly so. Had he not created more jobs than were ever held in the valley before? He says: "As long as the workmen are kept from idleness they will not think of unproductive theories to improve their status. They will keep their affairs in order and their houses clean, and will make enough money to support them in their old age. There is no other means of saving the people."

But his son Emile, though he does not doubt the permanent prosperity of his father's mills, raises an objection:

"What is this ideal of industry? To make the mass of the people toil incessantly for the benefit of a class which will never work at all?"

Cardonnet: "Oh, no, that is not the idea. I hate and despise idlers myself. Just as I dislike poets and metaphysicians. I should prefer that everybody work according to his capacity, and be remunerated according to his works. But the time is not ripe for such ideal changes. In the meantime we must help and serve the most capable among us so that he may have a chance to augment his wealth; for that is his duty, his religion, his philosophy."

Emile frowns on this gross materialism that expressed success in terms of money only and justified a system of ruthlessness, leaving the weaker members of society unprotected. Despising his father's money, he will not kneel to his gods. He wants to serve the higher needs of humanity. With this end in mind he marries the lovely and liberal-minded daughter of the carpenter Antoine and gladly inherits the millions and the communist library of a noble friend, Monsieur de Boisguilbaut.

George modeled her new heroes after her friends, Agricol Perdiguier, Poncy, and other artisan-poets who came daily to her house, much to the disgust of Chopin and the even more fastidious Solange.

These so-called proletarian poets had come into fashion some time before. They sprang from the artisan classes and were by no means representative of a political cause. Their verses expressed—often naïvely, often sublimely—nothing more than the joys and sorrows of the poor.

George had known Poncy and Perdiguier for some time and through their good offices met numerous others of the clan, among them Magu, an old weaver, deliciously naïve and ironic, and his son-in-law Gilland, a stanch Republican locksmith. Both became her lifelong friends.

George was always ready to advise and help them; they in return were devoted to her and her family. They approached her with modesty and also with confidence. The very tone of their letters gave proof of their high principles, their unselfishness, and their brotherly spirit. Gilland wrote to Madame Sand after he had been sent to prison for his revolutionary activities in '48:

"Dear kind Madame Sand! You are always the same to us, devoted, kind, and attentive as a mother or a sister. . . . Thanks many times for your double help, your letter and the money. I needed both. You will probably never realize what joy it is to me to read your message. The prison chaplain has lent me a volume of *The Fathers of the Church*. I am reading the chapter on Saint Bernard, which contains sublime pages. Well, I take up alternately Saint Bernard and your letter, and I derive greater joy from you. . . . He is too much of a saint. You have his greatness, knowledge, power to convince, and his humbleness before God, but you do not inspire fear; one would follow you anywhere. . . .

"I always imagine you to be Jean-Jacques Rousseau come back to earth, but I love you more than I do him, for he committed the one unpardonable sin—he abandoned his children.

"What is Maurice doing? He must become a great painter and then take me into his service to mix his paints and run his errands. . . . When I say I want to serve Maurice I am sincere. There will be no humiliating conditions in future society; whoever is useful to his brother will be respected for it, and will receive recognition. You may say that we are still far from such an ideal state, but I answer you with the

Gospel: Verily this reign has been established already among you! Have you not treated me as your equal? I eat your bread and you thank me for it. . . .

"Don't worry about sending me any more money. I get help from different sources, and once I am out of prison I shall find work again. But I promise that I shall turn to you in case I am in need. Adieu, Madame, trust in the future. Long live the Republic. Gilland."

If the proletarian poets profited by their famous friend, George in her turn profited no less—by an influx of new ideas and facts. Poncy taught her that the future would be in the hands of labor, and that the Republic would bring about a new renascence of the arts. Agricol Perdiguier gave her the material for her novel *The Journeyman-Joiner*, for he had himself written a book on the Brotherhoods in France.

Perdiguier believed that these Brotherhoods, also called Masonic trade unions, dated back to the temple-building unions under Solomon. The Christian stonemasons who worked in Jerusalem during the Crusades had simply re-adopted an old form of association which had been continued by the early Roman corporations and kept alive by Byzantine and Arab artisans. The labor associations which existed in France in the eighteenth and at the beginning of the nineteenth centuries were secret; though not acknowledged by law they were tolerated by the authorities. They took the title of *Devoirs* and—according to George—their chief, evidently their only, dogma was the principle of association. But each *Devoir* had its rites, insignia, and festivals —cause of jealousy and feuds between the rival groups.

George worked this material into the story of Pierre Huguenin, the journeyman-joiner. Pierre believes in equality and in the Republic which will put this principle into practice. But he despises the white-collar revolutionary who hails from the old Bonapartist (read: fascist) societies and aims at personal power, just as he despises the anarchical plotter of the Carbonaro brand who tells the workmen: "Agitate, excite, associate, arm! With that you can go anywhere!" On the contrary, Pierre urges the Brotherhoods to cultivate their sense of companionship and particularly to scorn the sense of rivalry among themselves:

"The feeling of a destiny common to all who work is revealed in me, and this barbarous custom of creating distinctions, castes, inimical camps between us all appears to me savage and fatal! Is it not enough that we have as natural enemy all those who exploit labor for their profit? Must we, while suffering from this inequality which casts us into the lowest rank, seek to consecrate inequality among ourselves? . . . We dispute the right of precedence in rival societies . . . we foolishly boast the antiquity of our origin, and we have not enough insults, threats, and outrages to hurl against the newly formed societies which seem to us stained by lowly origin and illegitimacy! . . . We provoke each other, cut each other's throats for the right to wear exclusively the square and the compass. As if every man who labors by the sweat of his brow had not the right to clothe himself in the insignia of his trade!"

But the meaning of the whole story lies elsewhere. George states it in her challenge to contemporary writers:

"Leave those heights on which the literary muse has so long kept herself apart from the great mass of the human race. Descend into those regions from which comic poetry draws so largely for the stage and the caricature. Deign to look upon the serious face of that pensive and deeply inspired people whom you believe to be still uncultivated and rude. You will see more than one Pierre Huguenin! . . . Look, I adjure you! Know his vices, for he has them . . .

but also know his greatness and his virtues, and as a result of your contact with him you will find yourself more artless and more generous."

She had learned her lesson well. Her pen had become a powerful medium for the spread of socialist propaganda. Her words traveled everywhere, battering with untiring energy the walls of the capitalist world.

In return, Mazzini, the fighter for liberty and national independence, gave her this beautiful foreword to her *Journeyman-Joiner:*

"And it is this which renders her [George Sand] doubly dear and sacred to us. She has suffered through us and for us. She has passed through the crisis of the age. The evil she pictures is not hers, it is ours. It does not come to us from her; it was and it is yet around us, in the air we breathe, in the foundation of our corrupt society, in the hypocrisy which has spread its ample cloak over all the manifestations of our life. But while we, partly from incapacity, partly from cowardice, have been silent at the risk of allowing the evil to become a fatal sore, she has spoken; she has with daring hand torn away the veil; she has laid bare the festering wounds and she has cried to us: *Behold your society!*"

CHAPTER SEVEN

The Nightingale Leaves

GEORGE'S private life through the 40's continued outwardly quiet and sedate. The family, including Chopin, had moved from the Rue Pigalle to a fashionable modern apartment house on the Square d'Orléans. George and Chopin had two apartments on the same floor, but Madame Marliani occupied the one intervening. When Pauline Viardot and her husband moved to the Square, all three families took their meals at Madame Marliani's. This arrangement lasted through the winters only; the summers were spent at Nohant as usual.

Solange was in boarding-school, Maurice a pupil at the studio of Delacroix. Chopin gave lessons, and his health seemed satisfactory except for an increasingly persistent cough. George worked hard at her books and articles. She found time to write long didactic letters to her friend Poncy, who had acquired the habit of praising the charms of strange houris rather than the chaste bosom of his wife or the future of the working-class.

173

Throughout the year 1843 she was busy launching a newspaper, the *Eclaireur de l'Indre*, which was to carry the Republican spirit into the very heart of France, or rather into George's native *département*. In order to make the foundation of the *Eclaireur* possible, George not only contributed money but carried on a vast correspondence with her friends and prospective editors and collaborators. Finally, in September 1844, she had the pleasure of seeing the first number published. She gave the journal nine articles, whose titles were expressive of their contents: "The Plight of the Paris Bakers"; "Letter from a Peasant of the *Vallée Noire*"; "Letter to the Editor in Behalf of a Petition for the Organization of Labor"; a critical account of Blanc's *Histoire de Dix Ans;* three articles on "Politics and Socialism"; etc.

Life on the Square d'Orléans was not much different from that in the Rue Pigalle. But foreign visitors who came to the house found George often rude and on the defensive, as if her character had begun to harden.

Gutzkow described his visit in 1842: "In a very small room . . . hardly ten feet square George sat near the fireplace, busy with her embroidery. Her daughter was opposite her. The tiny space around them was insufficiently lighted by a lamp with a very dark shade which barely permitted mother and daughter to see their needlework. Two men sat on a couch in another corner.

"Nobody introduced me as is customary in France. They were all silent, increasing the solemn, intimidating tension. I hardly dared to breathe; I felt choked; my heart refused to beat. The flame of the lamp trembled—the coal in the fireplace was reduced to pale ashes. The ghostly tick-tock of the clock was the only sign of life."

After a most unsatisfactory conversation in the course of

which George scarcely answered the questions put to her, Gutzkow, before leaving, threw a last glance at his ungracious hostess. He found her much like her famous picture by Charpentier, but thinner and somewhat sickly-looking. He likened her to a gazelle, and said she reminded him a little of Bettina von Arnim.

Lenz, a Russian writer and musician who had been introduced by Liszt, received a similarly cold welcome. He gave the following description of his visit to the Square:

"Finally it was possible to go and see Chopin. . . . *La cité d'Orléans* is a new building of large dimensions with a courtyard in the center . . . it is the first enterprise of its kind, with numbered apartments . . . situated behind the Rue de Provence in a very smart quarter. . . . Here where Chopin lived, Dantan, George Sand, and Pauline Viardot also had their apartments. At night they assembled at the flat of an old Spanish countess, a political emigrant who also lived in the building. All this was exactly as Liszt had told me. Chopin took me upstairs. He said: 'You will play something, but none of my things. Play that thing by Weber. . . .'

"George Sand did not say a word when Chopin introduced me. It was certainly not polite. But for that very reason I sat down beside her. Chopin fluttered about like a frightened bird in its cage; he saw something coming. . . . During a pause in the conversation, which was kept going by Madame Sand's friend Pauline Viardot, the great singer, Chopin took me by the arm and led me to the piano. . . . I played fragments from the 'Invitation à la Valse.' Afterward Chopin shook hands with me most amiably. George Sand did not say a word. Again I took my seat by her side, obviously pursuing a design of my own. Chopin regarded me across the table with much concern."

Those visitors who did not criticize George or Chopin, or

both, still found something to say about their relationship. Were they still in love with each other? Were they happy?

Mademoiselle de Rozières, a sharp-eyed spinster who was a friend of the family, made it her business to enlighten the visitors on this point: "There is no love between them, or at least only on one side. There is tenderness and loyalty, yes, but they are mixed up with regret, sadness, and boredom, caused by many things, but chiefly by the clash of two dissimilar temperaments."

What tortured the sensitive Chopin was the loud and graceless people who continually surrounded George, calling themselves her friends. Years before, Musset had been shocked by the impossible manners of her Berry friends. Chopin had still more reason to protest; he had more to put up with. He had to bear the crude gestures and words of the Poncys and Perdiguiers; shake hands with the repulsively untidy Leroux, whose collar was covered with dandruff; welcome Maurice's studio friends—a group of rude young artists who brought their pipes, dirty boots, and greasy coats into George's salon. At Nohant he suffered from the noisy drunkenness of George's half-brother, Hippolyte; in Paris he was bored by the proletarian half of George's family, Oscar Cazamajou, son of George's illegitimate half-sister Caroline, and also by Augustine Brault, a distant relative to whom George had offered the protection of her home because the young girl had a most disreputable hag of a mother. Oscar Cazamajou and Augustine were really quite charming and reserved, but they annoyed Chopin and Solange. Both refused to meet the "cousins" on an equal footing, and thus created a permanent source of dissension.

Chopin was pushed more and more into the role of a delicate, sensitive, and suffering wife, continually brutalized by a busy husband and his circle of coarse friends. He also complained that George was too cold, and that her lack of passion was killing him. George, however, insisted that his health made chastity imperative. But she wrote: "I have grown old before my time, without regret, without compulsion. I was disappointed and without hope, and tired of all passion."

Chopin was unhappy. Filled with a dark, seething jealousy, he became a source of continual suffering to himself and others. Often he was mute for days, made his "night-cap face," and ended up in a scene of dreadful hysteria. George somewhat callously described them in her new novel *Lucrezia Floriani:*

"Karol [Chopin] lay on his bed, his face pressed into the pillow. Cuffs and handkerchief were torn to pieces by his furious nails . . . his face was frightfully pale, his eyes bloodshot. His beauty had changed diabolically."

According to George, Chopin grew more and more bitter; he began to make scenes in front of everybody—her friends and her children. He was jealous of the gardener, the parish priest, a new servant, or even a face seen in the street. He seemed to hate the children and insisted that they were spoiled and ill-mannered. He was irritated by all the world.

And George! Her feelings were projected into the unfortunate Lucrezia—the heroine of her new novel:

"One day La Floriani was forty years old. . . . Suddenly she revolted against the fact that she had reached old age with its diseases and sufferings without being able to harvest its benefits as well—without having won her lover's confidence or respect, without his ceasing to regard her as his mistress rather than his friend. She sighed and told herself that she had striven in vain to inspire love in her youth and to win respect in her mature age. . . .

"Opposite her villa was a little olive wood which recalled

memories of her youth. Here, fifteen years ago, she had
given a rendezvous to her first lover. Here she had told him
for the first time that she loved him; here they had planned
their escape. . . .

"In her memory she recapitulated the incidents of her
first passion and compared them with those of her last love,
not in order to establish a cold comparison between the two
men, but to ask her heart whether it was still capable of suffering and passion. Rapidly she reviewed her whole life—
her attempts at devotion, her dreams of happiness, her disappointments, and her bitterness. She was shocked by what
her own life told her and wondered how she could possibly
have deceived herself so often without dying or going insane."

Poor George! Poor Chopin! We have never heard Chopin's side of the story. His letters and private papers were
destroyed. The few existing letters, addressed to George,
are disappointing in their dry and categorical tone. But
whatever his faults or drawbacks, Chopin suffered immeas-
urably more than George from the friction. Nor was his
health equal to the constant nervous strain. In 1844 he was
so ill that George, uneasy, asked his sister to come from Poland. Chopin's bitterness subsided somewhat when he found
himself reunited with a member of his family, but the happiness did not last. The final break between him and George
was precipitated by the children.

George's children had suddenly grown up. She had kept
them tied to her apron strings for years, educated them as
she saw fit, and led them successfully through the vicissi-
tudes of her life. At times they had been away from her,
under outside influences, with the result that they had
learned to view their mother more objectively. Probably
criticism had smoldered within them for a long time before it

burst into flame. Now, assuming their independence, they suddenly asserted themselves and began to dictate to their astonished parent.

There was little resemblance between brother and sister. Maurice was the physical and spiritual image of his mother, sharing her tastes and distastes, her opinions and gifts. He was an artist, though still merely a dilettante. He was orderly, subdued, and mildly egotistic. His ideas and activities fitted nicely into the comfortable pattern cut out for him by his mother's unceasing toil.

Solange was a much more complex person. In fact she was so full of contradictory traits that she seemed the meeting-place for all the extravagant characteristics of her ancestors. She was restless, critical, and utterly independent. Marie d'Agoult had said of the fourteen-year-old Solange: "She has a loving heart but a passionate and untamed character. . . . She is destined for the absolute in good and evil. Her life will be battle and strife."

At eighteen Solange was a beautiful girl with a great deal of spirit and wit, and a body of "wonderfully even proportions." But she was not a lovable person. She quarreled with everyone and terrorized the family. She was vain and impudent, and her fault-finding mind was forever on the lookout for victims. Not even her mother escaped criticism.

George did not realize that she was in a way responsible for the girl's difficult character. Maurice had always been the favorite, and Solange, "destined for the absolute in good and evil," had had reason to feel neglected. She would have liked to own her mother exclusively, yet had to stand back before Maurice, Chopin, and a crowd of indifferent people whom her mother called "friends." And so she hated her mother as she hated Maurice and the whole world—except

Chopin. Only dear Chip-Chop found grace in her eyes.
Solange and Chopin were indeed very intimate; they had
the same aversions and likes, and schemed and plotted constantly. He was a fellow-sufferer whom her mother neglected also, and whom her brother Maurice disliked. And
Chopin was elegant and well groomed, had rich and distinguished friends, was famous. Solange considered him her
natural and useful ally.

George tried to solve the difficult situation by marrying
off Solange. Chopin was not asked for his advice; he gave it
nevertheless. He demanded a seat and a voice at the family
council; Maurice refused him these rights. There were
scenes and finally Maurice's ultimatum: "Either Chopin
leaves or I do!" He knew the answer in advance.

George, however, was spared the decision. There was no
need to clothe her wish in the coarser form of language.
Chopin left on his own account. One cool autumn morning
he departed from Nohant—alone. Sick, coughing, wrapped
to his nose in woolen blankets, he looked back at George,
the children, and the house for the last time. Words of farewell were exchanged, hands waved, and then the coachman
took up the reins.

George did not hold him back, not now. A short separation seemed called for, though their friendly relationship
need not cease. But until Solange was married she would
prefer not to have an official lover in the house. The girl's
future must be considered. She had a dowry of one hundred
and fifty thousand francs, and a husband in secure circumstances must be found for her.

George for this purpose let her friends pass in review.
She would have liked Louis Blanc as a son-in-law; he was
an eminent historian and journalist, and she had known
him rather intimately since 1844. She liked his theories on

social reform; he had new ideas on employment and national relief, and a great influence with the working-classes. Some said he was the illegitimate son of Pozzo di Borgo, but that was not very likely. On the other hand . . . But Solange cut these speculations short—she refused. She was interested neither in Blanc's socialism nor in his undersized figure. Another suitor, Victor de Laprade, had more chance, but he was eliminated by the veto of his own family. The prize went finally to Fernand des Préaulx, a pleasant young man from the neighborhood who had the good fortune to please Solange. The engagement was officially announced. However, while George and her daughter were in Paris buying the trousseau, a young sculptor named Clésinger asked to model Madame Sand. The favor was granted. The bust may still be seen in a quiet corner of the Louvre; it shows a tired old woman with deep lines of suffering in her face.

Clésinger also modeled a bust of Solange, and in the course of the sittings fell in love with her. Solange reciprocated his feelings, broke her engagement with the rather unimportant young man in Berry, and ran away to be married to Clésinger. George gave her blessing when it was too late to do anything else. She did not like Clésinger, who was a former *cuirassier*, "a noisy gentleman who always caused confusion and behaved as if he were at the café or the military barracks." He had a violent temper and was head over heels in debt.

Shortly after the marriage the couple came to Nohant. There were scandalous scenes. Maurice and Clésinger attacked each other with hammers. The incident completed the break between George and her daughter. The following day George reported to Mademoiselle de Rozières, perhaps in the hope that the spinster would spread the gossip: "The

diabolical pair have left . . . covered with debt but triumphantly impudent and leaving behind a scandal that will not
easily be forgotten in the country. I don't want to see them
again. . . . My God, I have not deserved such a daughter!"

It was not the first scandal the country had known since
the descendants of the Maréchal de Saxe had come to live in
their midst. But the details of the story were more unsavory
than usual. They centered upon the young adopted cousin
of the Sands, Augustine Brault, who had become engaged
to one of Maurice's studio friends, Rousseau. Solange went
about insinuating that Augustine had been Maurice's mistress, and that Maurice was trying to rid himself of her by
marrying her to Rousseau. The engagement was then
broken off, though George tried to save the girl's reputation
by loudly proclaiming her innocence. Before long George
herself was accused of having fostered the affair between
Maurice and Augustine. As a result there was another quarrel—this time with Hippolyte, and in the end George's
honest, noisy, and really devoted half-brother left the house
too. He died a year later without having made an attempt at
reconciliation.

George wanted Chopin to remain in ignorance of the
difficulties, but he heard about them from Solange. He took
the daughter's side, and severed all relationship with Nohant. George tried in vain to win him back; she even wrote
to his family in Poland, but Chopin would not yield. "Even
cypresses have their moody moments," he said with bitterness. He met George once at the house of friends, and approached her only to tell her that Solange had a daughter.

George had forced the thorn deep into her nightingale's
heart and had driven him from her garden. Now the nightingale refused to return, but the thorn remained and the
heart was bleeding to death. The excitement, worry, and

suffering of the last years were destroying Chopin's delicate health. He had been unable to compose since he saw George last in the summer of 1847. All his energies were needed to fight the sickness of his soul and body. At the beginning of 1848 he gave one last brilliant concert in Paris, then went to England and Scotland for more triumphant recognition. But his resistance was worn down. Adoration, fame, even praise bestowed by the queen herself, exhausted rather than stimulated him. Only his outer appearance still concerned him: each day a valet "with the salary of a chief editor" curled his hair, and his clothes remained as immaculate and elegant as ever.

Occasionally he revealed his bitterness. To Grzymala he wrote: "I have never in my life condemned anyone; but everything seems so insupportable at the moment that it would be a help if I could curse 'Lucrezia.' "

In January 1849 he was back in Paris, seemingly improved and happier under the care of friends, but toward the end of the summer his strength failed rapidly. In October he was dying. On the thirteenth he received the last rites, and that evening said: "Now my agony begins."

One of his last requests was that Delphine Potocka should sing for him. He died on the seventeenth. His friend Franchomme thought he heard him whisper at the last: "And she promised that I should die in her arms."

But "she" was far away in Nohant. No one had told George of Chopin's desperate condition. At Nohant they were busy staging a puppet show.

CHAPTER EIGHT

Revolution

"LONG live the Republic!" George wrôte to Poncy on March 9, 1848. "What ecstasy, what enthusiasm, and at the same time what order and discipline in Paris! I have just hurried here, arriving while the last barricades were taken down. I have seen the great, sublime, naïve, generous French people united at last. I have seen it at one with the heart of France—with the heart of the world."

The people! It had been the hope and battle-cry of the reformers since the days of Rousseau. In its name mountains of paper had been wasted, rivers of blood shed. Barricades and systems had been erected and destroyed, authority abolished and re-established. But whoever had tried to lead this same people to supremacy had lost it on the way, and this had happened inevitably in the last fifty-five years. Whenever an attempt was made to establish the principles of liberty, equality, and fraternity in France, something quite different, something nobody had fought for, was in the end victorious. The restored authority had nothing to do with the people; its face was not proletarian, but middle class. In the decades after the French Revolution, not the people but the bourgeoisie came into power, nor was the victory complete for all of the bourgeoisie. The electoral laws of 1831 had given the franchise only to people who paid an income tax of two hundred francs a year or more, and made eligible for office only people with income-tax receipts of five hundred francs or more. These laws allowed 190,000 well-to-do Frenchmen to go to the polls, but reserved government offices for the higher class: the financiers, landowners, high officials, and members of the Academy.

The middle-class intelligentsia and the petty bourgeoisie were at a disadvantage under contemporary voting laws, yet they were capable of organizing an opposition movement.

Most of this opposition was still dynastic in its attitude. The number of actual Republicans, represented by the *National* and the *Réforme*, was small. No more than 2000 avowed Republicans were said to have been in Paris on the eve of the Revolution of '48. To these may be added 400 to 500 old conspirators and 1500 Polish, Italian, and Spanish refugees. All in all there were probably 4000 under the Republican banner in Paris. In the *départements* there were perhaps 15,000 to 16,000.

It is easy to be misled by statistics. There were not many Republicans, but certainly there were enough people who desired a change of government. Paris had an especially large proportion of the jobless, the shiftless, and the antisocial. A third of its population of a million was said to have been born out of wedlock. Brought up in foundling asylums or under the most outrageous social conditions, these children never acquired social virtues in the course of their handicapped careers. Many of them, the "scum of society," could easily be swept into a right or left revolutionary movement. To them revolution would afford a pleasant release in terror and bloodshed, and they would be only too glad to mount the barricades and fight society in any form.

It is certain, however, that the Republicans were not prepared for revolution, though they stirred up much unrest with their "reform banquets." But revolt and panic spread without them, owing to crop and weather catastrophes, and especially to the commercial and industrial crisis which had hit England and then spread to the Continent. Discontent and despair, seeking an outlet, found it on the day that the grand banquet of Paris was canceled by the police. The banquet, set for February 22, was to protest against the restricted vote. Guizot considered the banquet unnecessary, and the Republicans, obedient to the official word, had canceled the meeting. But the public had been too much aroused to settle back into its peaceful routine. It staged a demonstration of its own. On February 23 there was an *émeute* in the streets, and fifty people were shot down. After that the insurrection assumed the dimensions of a revolution. Before the day was over the king had been forced to dismiss Guizot and ask Thiers to form a new cabinet. But already the revolution had got ahead of him. The first red flag was hoisted over the barricades of Saint-Denis. By February 24 the king had abdicated and was off to England with his queen, traveling as Mr. and Mrs. William Smith. The mob of the Faubourgs forced the reluctant Republican leaders to the City Hall, and called for the proclamation of the Republic. Lamartine, in the Chamber, being deputized to name the members of the Provisional Government, appointed those whose names came first to his mind. Their rule lasted ten weeks, until the National Assembly had been voted for and the members of the Provisional Government had become a target for public ridicule.

To George and most of her friends the twenty-fourth of February had come as a surprise, although they had helped to prepare for the event for the last ten years. George was in Nohant writing *The History of My Life* and preparing a new edition of Rabelais, which was to be purged of all obscenities. Two days after the abdication of Louis-Philippe she had in her hands the membership list of the Provisional Government and found that most of her friends were included, among them Ledru-Rollin and Louis Blanc, who had been her collaborators on the *Réforme*. She closed her copy-books, put her pen back on the inkstand, ordered the family coach, and departed in haste for Paris.

Much of Paris had the charm and quiet aspect of a Biedermeier town. There were a few five-story buildings on the boulevards and small villas surrounded by gardens. Large trees lined the streets, giving ample shadow to the leisurely crowd below. Families with children sat sedately on chairs watching the luxurious carriages and elegant horsemen in the center of the Mall; others walked up and down and gossiped with their friends. All the way over to the Boulevard du Temple there was a pleasant assortment of cafés—the Café Anglais, the Café Américain, the Café de Paris, the Café des Variétés—offering an ice or a glass of beer to those tired of so much social activity.

When the revolution broke out, the calm and contentment of the average *flâneur* were greatly ruffled by the influx of proletarians from the suburbs. But his curiosity did not weaken. Streets and boulevards were more crowded than ever and looked as motley and gay as in the days of carnival. Everyone walked about looking for news, trying to find out what the Republic looked like. Young artisans, with tricolored or red rosettes in their buttonholes, walked arm in arm with their girls. The more courageous stopped to talk to Caussidière's men, who represented the Republican police. Though they had been recruited from among the revolutionary workers and members of secret societies they looked more picturesque than dangerous with their red-peaked caps, blue blouses, red sashes, and huge swords.

Even the conservative members of the bourgeoisie and the nobility mingled with the throngs, though they were cautious enough to wear soft hats or grow beards before venturing outside. On the whole the bourgeoisie did its best to conform. They sold their horses and let their servants go. They learned the political terminology of the revolutionary parties, and said that Proudhon was decidedly logical. They went out to fraternize with the workmen "because we are all more or less laborers." But in the privacy of their homes they looked aghast at the stock-exchange quotations, prayed for a quick ending to the terror, and consoled themselves with stories of atrocities and government graft.

Discontent with the new government was already rising. George, if she had walked among the street crowds, could have picked up much discouraging comment. Rothschild himself was quoted as saying: "*Rien ne vaut plus rien . . . que faire?*" Louis Blanc was a blundering fool, alienating the army. Caussidière and Courtais were drinking themselves to death and nightly could be picked out of the gutter. Ledru-Rollin was paying his debts with money collected for the wounded . . . and Minister Albert, a workman risen from the ranks, no longer considered himself a revolutionary now that he was earning ten thousand a year.

George, too, was the target of much animosity, particu-

larly from the conservatives who considered her the most
wicked of the extremists. They said: "Communism is a bug-
bear of little importance; its most dangerous point is having
George Sand as a mouthpiece," or: "Have you seen Ledru-
Rollin's last proclamation? He quotes Jean-Paul . . . and
says the finest fruits alone are attacked by wasps, and so he
alone of the Government has been attacked by calumny,
etc. . . . George Sand, of course, wrote this nonsense, because the Minister of the Interior is not poetic."

George had quickly assumed an active role in the new
government. Among its members she was closest to Ledru-
Rollin. He represented the petty bourgeoisie and the non-
communist laborers of Paris. He was not altogether a socialist, although he has been called so by the more conservative
historians. Only at the beginning of his career did he favor
social as well as political affranchisement. George said of
him at the time: "He is ours—that is, he belongs to the
people!"

Ledru-Rollin gave George a *laissez-passer* to all the min-
istries, and she at once found herself in the very center of
things. She talked to Lamartine at the Ministry for Foreign Affairs, visited Louis Blanc at the Luxembourg. Before long she was acting as Minister of Propaganda for
Ledru-Rollin. She drew up plans to further the revolution
in the provinces and wanted agents sent into the *départements*. As emissaries she recommended her labor friends,
since "they were trustworthy and because neither Reynaud,
Charton, nor Carnot knows good working-men in Paris."

To keep up the ardor and enthusiasm of the masses she
issued countless bulletins, articles, and proclamations. The
flow of her eloquence never ceased during those days:

"O people, gentle and powerful people, you are strong
because you are good! You are the best of friends, and

happy are those who have always given preference to you, have sacrificed their friendships and their material interests to you, have suffered ridicule for your sake, have prayed and grieved for you. . . . They are proud of you today, for your virtue has become visible to the world. Yours, O people, today as yesterday!"

The men in power were an honest group, but they were altogether too literary. Rhetoric can help make a republic, but will not keep it going. The government formulated its good intentions in too vague and disconnected a way. George had prophesied something of the sort in a letter to her friend Duvernet in 1841, when she said that vague benevolence would not suffice to republicanize the people. What was this people anyway? The Republicans, having come into power, realized with much surprise that it was not "the poorest and most numerous class" they had always discussed and written about, but the whole of the French nation, offering a most contradictory and unruly multiplicity of interests and classes.

George tried to solve the difficulty with an appeal to good will. Her "Letter to the Middle Class" contained the following words: "The Republic has come . . . it is the best and most beautiful form of human society. . . . The Republic which we are establishing will know only free and equal members. The system which we with the help of God destroyed made rich and poor equally unhappy. Each class considered the other as enemies. The poor feared the betrayal and tyranny of the rich, the rich the vengeance of the poor."

George, sure that the rest of the nation shared her ideals, left for Nohant on March 17, to help in the republicanization of Berry. But the country had been suspicious of benefits brought from Paris since the time of the departed Louis-

GEORGE SAND
Drawing by Couture *(Musée Carnavalet)*

Philippe. Innovations cost money, and the peasant would
not pay. "Long live the Republic, but down with taxes!" he
cried, as if he knew that these benign-looking Republican
emissaries were surely after his moneybag.

Nevertheless, in mid-March, Nohant had its Fete of the
Republic. The ceremony was touchingly described in the
Réforme. The peasants dashed up on their horses, rifles
across their saddles and the mantles of the National Guard
loose around their shoulders. They looked somewhat terrifying from afar, but the expression of their faces showed
them to be harmless, enthusiastic Republicans. They gathered in the little country church, which had been adorned
with violets, white primroses, and green branches. Women
and children carried flags and flowers. A solemn mass was
said for the dead of the Republic, after which the crowd
moved in unison to the village, where a "liberty" tree was
planted and the new tricolored flag raised. The sound of
drum and bagpipe mingled with the cheers of the eager
crowd. The priest blessed the flag, and the country officials
—with Maurice Sand as the newly elected mayor—stood
by with their heads uncovered. The dawn of humanity
prophesied by Rousseau was indeed rising above the horizon, and Madame Sand had proved that she knew how to
advertise the Republic.

After her return to Paris, George was much pained to
see that the members of the government were at odds with
one another. They had decreed universal franchise, increasing the number of voters to nine millions, and the new elections were fixed for the middle of April; they had promised
a new educational system and guaranteed the freedom of
the press. Small pawns had been released free of charge;
corporal punishment in the Navy was abolished. Numerous
other decrees gave proof of the humanitarian spirit of the

government. But a definite policy had not been agreed upon. Ledru-Rollin, politician of the deepest dye, tried to mediate and conciliate in every direction. But the trouble was that each of the members had his own scheme and would not agree to that of his neighbor. The dissension was fed by the clubs, which sprang up like mushrooms after rain. They bred phrases and extravagant proposals, dreams and ambitions far removed from the needs of the moment. The only group which accomplished work was the Commission of the Luxembourg, which consisted of delegates from the corporations of Parisian artisans and was presided over by Louis Blanc. They were charged to find a means of organizing labor and production. Louis Blanc preached the National Ateliers, but the workshops opened by the government under the direction of Minister Marie had little in common with Blanc's ideal. They were not a congregation of specialized artisans running a shop with money of their own, but public workhouses, paying the unemployed two francs a day for tedious unproductive labor.

Among the members of the government Louis Blanc was probably the one best equipped mentally to carry through a reform of the country. Proudhon said that Blanc was inwardly convinced of the necessity for dictatorship, but lacked the courage to establish it. "What is liberty to starving men!" Blanc had once exclaimed. His ideal was the establishment of a popular government with great power of initiative. The state could then regulate industry, since competition had failed to provide for workmen security of employment. Blanc thought that ultimately all individual enterprise would be eliminated, and as a preliminary step toward that end he advocated socialization of banks, mines, and railroads. He tried to teach a sense of responsibility to all social classes, but chiefly to the workers. Work does honor to the workman, he said. To be a worker means to participate in social glory. The workman is the soldier of the state, and his attitude toward society must no longer be dictated by egotism and material interest.

George, who agreed ideologically with Louis Blanc, tried to get away from the phrase, and to come face to face with reality. The formal bulletins she edited for the government were being sent to all the communities in France and the mayors were obliged to post them on the church doors.

Maurice Sand thus found himself under the happy obligation of proclaiming his mother's word to his district. George, highly gratified by this fact, wrote him in addition: "Read it [the bulletin] to the National Guard, slowly and distinctly. This will flatter them. Explain to them the necessity of the tax. Try to republicanize them further. We have enough wine in the cellar. Treat them to it, but with discretion, and in the kitchen." However, La Châtre organized a counter-movement, and an excited mob marched to Nohant, crying: "Down with Madame Dudevant! Down with Maurice Dudevant! Death to the communists!"

These private persecutions did not much affect George; they were part and parcel of the business of revolution. Immediately she advised Ledru-Rollin to fight this counter-movement. All her labor friends—the Poncys, Gillands, Magus—were called upon for co-operation and departed for the provinces. The elections of April 23 had to be thoroughly prepared; only reliable Republicans should appear on the ballot. The slogan was: Only yesterday's Republicans can be those of today!

Someone suggested to George that she avail herself of the services of Michel de Bourges, but George refused to ask his aid. "Let him try for a mandate some other time, not now. At the moment we need more reliable men. When the Republic needed him he was not there." George had not forgotten, though it was years ago, that Michel had turned his back on the Cause and returned to his wife and the easy duties of a government post. She avenged herself by a simple stroke of the pen. But did not the safety of the Republic demand it?

The government was indeed in a desperate plight; the treasury was empty, savings accounts limited to withdrawals of one hundred francs. Banknote values were fixed by fiat. A surtax of forty-five per cent had been added to the direct land tax, which fell chiefly on the peasant, owner of nine-tenths of the country's real estate. Together with the bourgeois, he protested against this new burden, and declared that his money was going for the relief of the unemployed and the upkeep of the national workshops. "Are we not paying some sort of strike insurance for the workmen?" he asked himself.

The conservative elements, supported by the Bonapartists, had started the counter-movement. George declared angrily in her bulletin that if the coming elections proved a disappointment, the result had to be annulled by asking the people to vote again.

"What!" cried the bourgeoisie. "Is franchise not the wonder-cure for all our ills? Then what did we get it for?" George's somewhat careless declamation sent the moderates into an uproar, and the government was heavily attacked for having let the article pass uncensored. "You encourage the mob," it was told.

The sixteenth of April brought more shocks. The radical clubs had prepared an insurrection which was to oust the more moderate government members and install the dictatorship of Ledru-Rollin, with Blanc and Barbès as his supporters. Blanqui meanwhile made a move for communist rule. Fortunately the government was on its guard and quickly quelled the rebellion with the help of the National Guard. Lamartine was the hero of the day, and there were laurels too for Ledru-Rollin, who had successfully extricated himself from a somewhat dubious situation. The Paris mob was ready to cry: "Death to the communists! Death to the socialists! Down with Cabet!" The bourgeoisie recovered its courage and began to advocate more reactionary measures. George wrote to her son: "I am afraid the Republic is done for, at least some time soon."

Marie d'Agoult, who under the pen-name of Daniel Stern wrote a *History of the Revolution of 1848*, accused George of actual participation in the April plot:

"Madame Sand was one of the most active agents of the conspiracy, less in the interest of Ledru than in that of Louis Blanc. She had brought Barbès into it, and tried to win over the workmen who gathered in her small apartment every night. Later in the evening she would join the small circle of guests at the Ministry of the Interior, where Favre, Landrin, Carteret, Etienne Arago, and Barbès were present. With or without Ledru-Rollin they would discuss the means of getting back into power."

But the reins of the Republic remained where they were, at least for the time being. And George could not help confessing: "It is better to support the Provisional Government than to become a victim of Blanqui and Company."

In the meantime she had to fight a conspiracy of another kind—the conspiracy of women! A few socialist ladies had formed a club of their own, and were advocating the franchise for women.

Flaubert gave a picture of the suffragette of '48 when he described Mademoiselle Vatuaz in his *Education Sentimentale:*

"She was one of those Parisian women bachelors who come home every night tired and with their skirt-hems soiled after having taught all day, or tried to sell their little oil paintings or their pitiful manuscripts. They cook their dinner, eat it by themselves, a hot-water bottle under their feet, and by the light of a dreary lamp dream of family, love, a home of their own, and money—of all the things lacking in their lives. When the Republic was proclaimed she greeted it as the day of vengeance, and joined in a frantic socialist propaganda. She wanted to enter every profession, demanded legal paternity for the illegitimate child, and other and better marriage laws. Each Frenchwoman was to marry a Frenchman, or adopt an old man. Nurses and midwives were to be civil-service employees. There was to be a special jury for all women's art, a women's polytechnical school, a women's national guard, everything for women."

A Club des Femmes had been formed and it had two candidates, Legouvé and—George Sand. George was furious at having been drawn into such a ridiculous candidacy and refused the offer. Her letters to the ladies in question gave her reason: "Women, especially when married, are not ready to vote, not so long as they are morally and economically dependent on men." She went on to show that even most men were not mature enough to vote, and that it was unlikely women would show more wisdom and dignity under the circumstances. In fact, they would only increase the existing confusion. George, who had assumed the task of educating the male population in democracy, refused to enlighten the other half of the population too. "It seems to me that those socialist ladies mistake equality for identity when they want to be like men in the future. . . . Man and wife have their different functions without woman's being inferior to man."

Busy preparing the elections, she could give no further attention to their petty claims. Her proclamations, articles, and letters of the next weeks are one urgent prayer to the people to elect steadfast Republican candidates.

"The sovereignty of the people must be assured under all circumstances. The people have the right to be sovereign; God Himself gave this right in creating all men equal. . . .

"Sovereignty means equality for all, therefore sovereignty can have its seat only with the people. Sovereignty of the people means power for all. That is their right; their duty is to exercise this right. . . .

"Socialism is the goal, the Republic is the means. . . . Universal equality must replace class rule; competition and monopoly must yield to association and co-operation. . . . What is the bourgeoisie afraid of? Inheritance tax, revolutionary measures, enforced contributions, socialization of the means of production, our troubles and needs for which they must make amends? If they fear these things let them have sleepless nights, for it is certain that they must make sacrifices."

In the end she relented: "All this will not come to pass suddenly and through force, but by slow evolution. . . . For the moment society will only prevent the formation of scandalous fortunes. Slave labor and usury will be curtailed. . . . If the poor must have patience for a while, they know that the government will meet their demands at the earliest moment possible. The rich must, however, not be too rapidly expropriated. Misery would demoralize them to such a degree that they would physically and mentally perish and become a new problem for the Republic."

But the bourgeoisie did not understand George's language. They insisted that terror and murder were behind her promises. If a peaceful reform was desired, let them go ahead with the capital tax! Let them proclaim the worker's right to work and watch the result.

The right to work, to find employment! It meant the destruction of wage labor and capital and their mutual relationship; it implied the confiscation of capital, the expropriation of all means of production and their subjection to the united workers. The bourgeoisie of 1848 could not formulate the consequences as clearly as Marx did later on, but it suspected some of them. It did not like Madame Sand's program or that of her friends. It voted against it, and so did the mass of the people, who were afraid of more experimenting and confusion. As Briand once said, "The Frenchman easily adopts a revolutionary attitude, but just as quickly abandons it again. What he essentially wants is economic security for himself, his family, and the nation at large." France, after weeks of insecurity and political and economic confusion bordering on panic, was tired of the experiment and voted for peace and reaction.

The election of May 4 proved "a living protest against the presumptions and aspirations of the February days." Not one socialist was able to secure a seat in the government.

As soon as the newly elected National Assembly had met, George addressed a letter of flaming protest to her former friend Lamennais, who had introduced into the constitution a paragraph conveying the executive power in France to a president elected for a period of three years. "The authority of a single individual is contrary to the ideas and feelings of the masses, and would be a signal for a civil war. . . . The president would be forced to become a dictator, and every dictator wades in blood."

Her tone still sounded militant, but her enthusiasm was subdued, and the faith that had moved mountains seemed gone. Of the insurrection of May 15 she knew nothing beforehand. She had no part in the attacks on the Chamber and City Hall by the revolutionary workers, who demanded a billion francs in taxes and the dissolution of the National Assembly. Immediately after May 15 she returned to Nohant, while the government started a purge and proceeded with the systematic suppression of all radical elements. The communist leaders were arrested; so were many socialists. Blanc was faced with an official investigation. George was accused of conspiracy, and there were cries for her arrest. But Ledru-Rollin, still a member of the executive committee, gave her a safe-conduct to Nohant.

George's political role was finished. The press saw no more of her revolutionary articles and proclamations. Possibly her silence was a voluntary one, because she had realized that she would do better to spin the thread of her imagination in fiction than in politics.

"We have gone in for too much old-fashioned journalism," she confessed. The people, she thought, were not ready to govern themselves; the very fact that they chose their representatives from among the bourgeoisie showed their lack of self-confidence and maturity. But it seemed impossible to her that a single man could ever be superior to a principle. "The only principle of vital consequence to future society is and will always be—democratic representation! Only the peaceful and legal struggle between the different political factions will show the people what it wants and what it needs."

George heard of the June massacres only from others. They roused such horror in her that she hardly dared comment on them in her letters. The people—her "strong and gentle people"—had gone into an orgy of destruction. Ten thousand were killed or wounded. Prisoners were shot down wholesale; unheard-of atrocities committed on the wounded. One of the last victims was the Archbishop of Paris himself, who had gone to the barricades with the hope of mediating between the insurgents and the army. Thousands were jailed or deported. The losses were all in all greater than those of many Napoleonic battles.

Cavaignac, who had put down the insurrection after a three-day struggle, became military dictator of Paris, and remained in power for four more months. But Paris had resumed its peaceful pace even earlier. Baroness Bonde, a gossip-mongering Swedish woman who had lived through the whole of the Paris revolution, wrote friends in London on July 27 : "There is a slight tendency toward commercial improvement, and the theaters, which had been closed for three weeks, are full every night. I was at the Palais Royal on Tuesday and saw a delightful burlesque of the Republic, besides some of the charming trifles which have '*un succès de fou.rire*.' "

The revolution had cost the country ten billion francs.

PART THREE

Compromise

"Nach innen geht der geheimnisvolle Weg."

—Novalis

CHAPTER ONE

Return to the Lambs

G EORGE was back in Nohant.
The pale sky and the mild air of Berry were a pleasant antidote for the bitter experiences of the revolution.

"Oh, for the utter mildness of the native sky . . . the
peace of quiet waters . . . the gracious silence of the wind
in the tree-tops!"

The country seemed lovelier than ever, and George with
her plant-box slung over one shoulder went strolling across
the meadows in search of some rare beetle or plant. At noon
she took a swim in the river or rested under the willow
trees. What more could she ask for than the sight of green
horizons and calmly grazing cattle, the sound of rippling
waves or stirring leaves, the faint little cry of millwings
turning in the distance? They made her forget the confusion and horror of the recent past; they covered up personal
memories that cut deeper still: the sight of a carriage leaving Nohant park, inside that carriage a sick man wrapped
in blankets, bidding her farewell with a tired gesture.

She will not yield herself to thoughts that weaken and sadden her; she will turn toward the positive in life: to the beauty in nature and all the lovely things that God created. She will draw strength and wisdom from her immediate environment, the hills and trees and the river by her side, yes, even from that caterpillar there that has fallen into the water. She must toss it a leaf so that it may save itself. George hates to see a living thing suffer, even an unattractive one like a caterpillar.

She murmurs: "If all ugly things were killed, how could we ourselves survive?"

She watches the flow of the water, thinks of the many little things around her, each with a lesson to teach. She studies the miserable weeds at her feet. "Look," she tells herself, "they are full of beneficial qualities, yet we disdain them because they are small and dismal. Why can't we forget our pride that makes us eternally turn toward the exotic, the impressive, the grandiloquent, the heroic? Why don't we ever learn the truth from the humbler things in life? Is it because we ourselves are not big enough for the small things?"

She remembers—rather uneasily—her long bombastic tirades in *Horace* and *Consuelo*. Well—that was past history. From now on her inspiration will come from the lowly and humble, from the herbs and caterpillars, from the clouds and trees and the modest ways of the peasant.

For a while she continues to muse over those things that are gentle and kind and that still the anxiety of her heart. She watches the men laboring in the fields, or driving their teams of oxen home over the roads.

The men sing to make the oxen move more rapidly.

"Holé, holé, holé, my boy!
    Holé, holé, my two little brothers, my pretty one!"

They know no more than a few haphazard words, and
the melody too is always the same. It is very old and comes
out of a past that knew the arts of magic. The secret was
lost now, but the peasant still believed in the power of his
song to make his oxen work.

Much of the Berry tradition and custom was as old as
these songs, dating back to the times when the Romans,
even to when the Celts, ruled Gaul.

George's restless mind notes, compares, speculates. Had
not Leroux taught her that behind the contemporary face of
a race exists a more ancient and fundamental one, anchored
in the dreams and fears, needs and desires of a more primi-
tive humanity?

She will write about this ancient face of Berry, try to
preserve some of its older cultural elements in a series of
sketches, in a group of pastoral novels. She will bring into
the stories her early neighbors—the Fanchons, Sylvains,
and Germains, their weddings and harvests and deaths and
age-old struggle for their daily bread. The walk in the
country today was helpful; it has given her new ideas. Tonight she will start on a new story and call it *La Petite
Fadette*. It will be a story of peasant life and have no political implications. The new government has no need for humanitarian proclamations and, besides, the new censorship
would make them impossible.

The book was dedicated to her friend Barbès, now impris-
oned in Vincennes; its foreword was published in the *Spec-
tateur Républicain* under the title, "Why We Return to Our
Lambs." It explained why from now on Madame Sand

would confine herself to art. "Art will compensate for any ruins!" Art and the beauties of nature offered the one possible escape from the disappointments of political life. In singing the praise of nature and poetry, George hoped to bring a little consolation to a much suffering humanity.

Nohant continued to be a quiet place in the years after 1848. George had leisure enough to meditate on the changes in world affairs. Her books did not sell so well and her budget was much reduced.

Political pressure on the liberals increased in intensity rather than subsided. Louis Napoleon, who had become President of the Republic in December 1848, quickly revealed his original intention of ruling the country with an iron hand.

This nephew of the first Napoleon had during the long weary years of his pretendership capably prepared for his ultimate role as dictator of France. Two men had helped him along his road to success: Fialin, who later called himself Duc de Persigny, and his own half-brother, Charles de Morny, an offspring of Queen Hortense and the Count of Flahaut. Fialin, a soldier and a journalist, had organized the Bonapartist propaganda before '48. With the help of two other gentlemen devoted to the Bonapartist cause, he had come to Paris and worked on French public opinion in the usual manner. He distributed portraits of the prince and labeled him "Savior of France." He won the small bourgeoisie, particularly the small tradesmen, by promising them a more splendid future. He had a newspaper, used printed posters, and even hired street-musicians to spread the Bonapartist gospel. He had organized the remnants of the Grande Armée—the Ratapoils—into something like a private militia. There was not much glamour left in Napoleon's former veterans, but their fighting spirit was still powerful enough to make them brandish their big sticks and terrorize the streets with their songs.

However, the overwhelming vote that had swept Louis Napoleon into presidential power had come about through the most contradictory elements. The Monarchists thought he would be too weak to keep his position when elected, and would thus prepare the way for the Bourbons. The Catholics chose him because he was a personal friend of the Pope. The rural population voted for him because the 45 per cent surtax of the revolutionary government still rankled. The working-men supported him out of their hatred for the bourgeoisie. Others thought he was a ship in an uncharted sea and might lead them to a new and miraculous port.

Other factors contributed to make him popular: Victor Hugo with his heroic verses and Béranger with his popular songs both glorified the Napoleonic legend and incidentally any heir to the Napoleonic tradition. Concerning Louis Napoleon's popularity in 1848 Victor Hugo had this to say in his diary:

"The superstitious favor Monsieur Louis Napoleon is enjoying these days must be interpreted as France's touching appeal to God: she needs a man to save her. . . . The name of Bonaparte can never become insignificant. Providence owes it to itself to guard its glory. Not only Monsieur Louis Napoleon must keep it great, but God Himself!"

And Louis Napoleon set out to save France. By the end of 1849 he had elected his own ministry and become his own prime minister. Freedom of vote and assembly was restricted, freedom of the press abolished—the latter by means of the "caution money" that every newspaper had to deposit. The book trade was even more strictly super-

vised: book-sellers and printers had to secure government
licenses; no book could be issued without the placet of the
censor. By 1851 the legislative body no longer had power
to amend laws, only to accept those submitted by the President.

But owing to the upward trend in business and trade,
which Louis Napoleon had himself predicted for his regime,
the people remained content. They had pawnshops and land
banks, and the telegraph appeared. France was rapidly becoming industrialized; she was growing prosperous.

Much as George might deny it, Louis Napoleon's name
exerted its fascination even upon her. It was bound up
with her childhood memories, with the image of her
father who had fought the battles of the Republic and became lieutenant the day the battle of Marengo was won.
Those distant happenings had their luminosity still. George
was of course too good a Republican to betray her ideals for
so small a cause. She could offer no allegiance to the new dictator of France, yet she could tolerate him. "He, too, had his
dreams of the glory of France."

Yes—she remembered the time when he was a prisoner
at Ham. He had written her charming letters: "Believe me,
Madame, that the most beautiful title you may give me is
that of a friend, for it proves a degree of confidence which I
should like to see established between us." He was then considered a rather foolish young pretender who had forfeited
his chances by an ill-prepared insurrection. Nobody would
have staked a penny on his future career. And yet—that
was only a few years ago. Not even Thiers had foreseen his
dictatorship; he had thought him a weakling. Before the
young man's election as a deputy, Thiers had advised that
he at least shave off his ridiculous mustache.

But from the beginning, when George had corresponded

with him on politics and economics, she had considered him
—perhaps misleading, but sincere. She could do something
now. She could at least try to stay the persecution of the
liberals.

Many of her friends had either been arrested or had fled
the country. Her dear Barbès was in prison. Leroux, Louis
Blanc, and Ledru-Rollin lived in exile in England. Others
were on the way to Devil's Island. She sent money to Gilland, and to that young German refugee in Paris, Dr. Muel-
ler, whom she wanted to come to Nohant for a while. What
irony that a German liberal, escaping his own country's
revolution, could find refuge in France while the French
liberals must hide abroad!

Even she herself feared arrest. Shortly before the *coup
d'état* in 1851, when Louis secured for himself the presi-
dency for life, she wrote to the almighty Carlier, former
police president of Paris, asking for a passport. The passport
was denied for formal reasons, but she received a letter from
the Paris police: "Madame Sand has permission to travel
freely from La Châtre to Paris."

The moment George arrived in Paris she sought an interview with the Prince-President.

"I want to explain my conduct," she said, "and ask him
frankly whether he will send me into exile. Deportation
would mean death to me. I am dangerously ill with liver
trouble and could never cross the sea alive."

But she quickly realized that nobody wanted to deport
her. On the contrary, the leading men in the government
were most cordial to her and the Prince-President granted
her an immediate interview.

When George went to see him, she took a long explana-
tory letter with her in case she should be too overcome to

talk to him in a composed manner. But the interview passed very pleasantly. George left the President impressed again with his sincerity. She also called on the Minister of the Interior, Morny, and wrote to Persigny for the same reason. She established contact with the President's younger cousin, Jerome Napoleon, who took her petitions to the highest authority.

"I keep running in every direction," she wrote to Duvernet. "Everything goes well. I could not have been more graciously received with handshakes and what-nots. Tomorrow I shall try to attend to your affair. The Gaulois [Fleury] and others down there abuse me and forbid me to plead in their favor. They are silly indeed, if they fear some foolishness on my part! But let them plead for themselves! There are enough others who would like to benefit in their stead."

Her efforts were not always welcomed by her liberal friends. In fact Fleury and his associates openly abused her when she tried to intervene on their behalf. They denounced her as a traitor to the cause. Another friend, Marc Dufraisse, wrote warningly from his exile in Belgium:

"He [Louis Napoleon] will reinstitute feudalism through his high-paid functionaries. He does not want independent entities within the state, and in order to dominate the nation he would gladly give an income to everyone.

"With time and listlessness supporting him, he will conquer us all with his militarism and red-tape. France will be a huge military barracks. He will suppress all activities as he has silenced all voices. Those who do not march with the rest will be considered bad citizens. He will give us the subserviency of communism combined with the social injustices of the present-day regime. Pretending that all ends must tend toward the welfare of the people, he will kill all courage because it is rebellious, and destroy all genius because it is factional. Everybody must keep within the ranks, but in order to bend the heads of the proud rather than reduce the bellies of the overfed. He will respect the country's material interests in order to be free to persecute noble and independent minds. The enfranchised are to serve him and the slaves to greet him. He loves the people no better than Caesar loved the plebs. . . . He will not destroy the capitalist aristocracy. He is after the aristocracy of the mind—the superior intelligence! It took the sad experience of our present-day politics to make me understand what Tacitus meant when he said: *'Magna ingenia et virtutes cessere!'* Apply this to the future and you will know what this man is preparing for us."

But George did not feel so pessimistic about the future. "Individuals, even leading individuals, have no real importance in the long run of history," she had written to a friend only the day before. She penciled underneath Dufraisse's letter: "I am more loyal than you, my friend!"

To others she said: "The President is an unfortunate victim of the belief that the end justifies the means. He thinks he is above the situation, but he is half submerged already. He no longer knows what he is doing . . . his cause is as lost as ours." But she still had faith in him. When she heard that in Châteauroux some of the arrested liberals had been dragged through the streets in chains she settled down to a long letter. In her large, naïve handwriting she told him this:

"They have left for the fortress in Bicêtre—those hapless prisoners of Châteauroux, condemned to deportation. Covered with chains they were led through the streets while the people stood by and wept. No doubt someone has told you that this would make a good impression. Why must you be deceived? . . . Why this severity, this terror, this denial of all human dignity and rights, this political hatred that destroys all notions of the true and the just? . . . Let me plead for mercy for these unfortunate men. I will plead on my knees and this will not humiliate me. God has given you absolute power; well, then—I am begging God as well as you, my friend of old!"

It was a long letter, interrupted by an occasional cigarette, and her tears.

CHAPTER TWO

The Theater and Madame Sand

FRANCE in the 50's became a great and powerful nation. In the eyes of all Europe it had regained whatever prestige had been lost under Bourbon or Orléans rule. Paris became a popular excursion center for European monarchs and princes, who went to the French metropolis for its world fairs and other attractions. Even Victoria, accompanied by the Prince-Consort, came to Paris in 1855 to visit the Exposition and to bring about a permanent alliance between France and Great Britain. Louis Napoleon had become Napoleon III. Victoria was charmed by the French Emperor's quiet and pleasant manners and delighted by her new intimacy with England's former foe.

With French popular interest focused on prosperity and political prestige, the business man, the well-to-do citizen, became a symbol of the nation's greatness and wealth. Economic expansion made him powerful and contented. It also stilled the restless ambitions of the working-classes, as there was employment for all. Monsieur Cardonnet had rightly predicted: "As long as the workmen are kept from idleness they will not think of unproductive theories to improve their status."

The nation was satisfied with its dictator. All political passions had subsided; all other passions too, except that for money. The trend was toward morality and the ethics of Protestantism, with its emphasis on sobriety, its sense of reality, and its healthy respect for earthly possessions.

Yet this glorification of the bourgeois soon prepared his downfall and decay. The foundation of prosperity had been the great middle-class virtues of a former generation: economy, honesty, simplicity, respect for tradition, and slow and honest toil. But these qualities were quickly forgotten in the feverish rush for gold which stirred all classes now. The business standards of old, which had made for solidity and sound value, had given way to mad speculation and doubtful policies. The day belonged to the ruthless profiteer, the smart business man, the clever hypocrite who outwardly conformed but sinned behind drawn curtains. The bourgeois ideal, still being held up to the public as a pattern, had long since gone out of their existence. The false front had no worth, no potentiality, no power to sustain those who tried to lean against it.

Nevertheless this front overshadowed all activity and speech, making art and literature subservient to its standards. Dumas *fils*, Sandeau, and Octave Feuillet were now hailed as the representatives of true and honest art, while Victor Hugo, Musset, and Gautier were frowned upon for their ambiguous aesthetics. They belonged to that doubtful generation which had lived in unconventional intimacy with the *grisette* of the Latin Quarter, and believed in ideals and love. Their art was considered as lawless as their morality, tainted with the Red Menace.

Love for its own sake could no longer be tolerated. Marriage, yes, marriage was sacred; illegal relationship between the sexes must not be acclaimed. The *grisette*, who sacrificed her doubtful virginity with ardor and unselfish enthusiasm, had no place in the present society. She had been succeeded by a less agreeable type—the *lorette*, who had her stucco and gilt apartment on Montmartre. The *lorette* lived on the fringe of society, her existence was denied, though sometimes, as in Dumas's *La Dame aux Camélias*, she was wept over on the stage. But she was not mentioned in the same breath with one's lawful wife; a gentleman refrained from taking off his hat in her presence.

George had often discussed the new trend with her friends. She might have found it easy to adapt her art to a more severe moral standard. She was a moralist herself and had declared that virtue—virtue born of love—was the uppermost law in human society. To differentiate good and evil, to punish the wicked and reward the virtuous, was an old weakness of the author George Sand, who had sadly missed such sentiments in the works of Balzac and Goethe. But the spirit of morality that ruled the arts now was no inspiration to George, for it was a spirit born of the most prosaic egotism. And there was no real virtue—not even bourgeois virtue. Nor was there any need for such demarcations as former society had known: bourgeois, artist, artisan, dreamer, fool and Bohemian, rich and poor, good and bad.

"Open your eyes," George told her friends. "All former notions, habits, and destinies have been shuffled like cards in the hand of a skillful gambler. . . . Things and men have changed. Who are the rich and the poor nowadays? Toil, trading, economy, wise calculation, and common sense used

to pave the way to wealth and security. But now it is hazard, fashion, audacity, chance, popularity which decide
one's destiny. The bourgeois you have in mind does not
exist any more. To make money or escape poverty the man
must no longer toil with patience, display the virtues of
the honest tradesman, or let himself be inspired by true
art; he must understand the technique of the banking system, must be able to calculate his financial chances, must
risk a daring coup, place his stakes well; in a word, he must
know how to gamble, because gambling has become the
heart and soul of modern society."

In a way George had become more anti-bourgeois than
ever. She explained it as a sensible reaction against the
speculative spirit and gross materialism of the day. She
suffered from this materialism; it stifled her. Nor was she
allowed to counterbalance it with any of her former idealistic theories. Her long-standing claims for social justice
had been silenced by the censor. It was a difficult day for
Madame Sand. She was too much of a socialist, too much
of an artist, to be one without the other. Her work grew trite,
colorless, and seemed far removed from actuality. The public did not read her much. While France was growing rich,
George was growing poor. In her need she turned to the
theater.

George had always had an ambition to write for the
stage. Her fascination for the theater went back to her
youth in the early 30's when she had dressed as a man
in boots, mixing with the crowd down in the parterre. In
those days she had for a long time been fascinated by the
great Romantic actress of the day, Dorval. She remembered
her best in Dumas's *Antony* and Vigny's *Chatterton*. The
actress's style had been admirably suited to the exigencies

of their plays; she wept and choked, tore her hair, lay writhing on the floor. Her voice seemed to master the range of all human emotions: it whispered, spoke, cried, and broke in joy and despair. Her pale blond hair, her frail limbs, the high delicate forehead gave her the sweetness and delicacy of an early Christian martyr. Dumas and Vigny loved her, and she had been Musset's last mistress. George had seen much of her in those years, so much that Vigny had become jealous of their intimacy.

In the 40's George had tried her hand at the stage with the play *Cosima*. Dorval created the title role, but it failed badly, for by this time the great actress's career was on the downward path. A few years later she was dying of tuberculosis, a woman without hope or ambition.

After the failure of *Cosima* George had been discouraged, but then Maurice suggested that she build an amateur stage in Nohant and try her plays on it before letting them go to the Odéon or the Gymnase. He felt certain that, with a first-rate cast and a well-trained claque behind her, the Paris public—always in search of first-night sensations—would gladly accept the latest literary contributions from Madame Sand.

The stage was built and the plays were taken from her novels, an experienced hack-writer adapting them to the requirements of the theater. Thereafter *François le Champi* was a mild success at the Odéon in 1849, *Le Mariage de Victorine* and two others were generously applauded at the Gymnase. A little later George caused a sensation with *Claudie* performed at the Théâtre Porte St.-Martin. The public relished the plot as a forbidden fruit, because it introduced proletarian and peasant characters to the stage. Yet the police had expurgated the text before it was produced and had eliminated such insidious remarks as: "Justice will be done; God has promised it," and: "The sheaf of wheat is the pillow of the people."

George was delighted with her success.

She enjoyed it for many reasons: for the success it gave her, the money it brought her, the generous sympathy she derived from the actors, and the new stimulus bound up with the eerie theatrical atmosphere. She was usually present for the rehearsing of her plays, and loved those long nightly vigils at the theater while actors and extras moved across the scene, apparently without plan or co-ordination. Groups of peasants or soldiers in white and in blue blouses would be sent on the stage, be off again, following some incomprehensible orders of a hoarse, feverish, and over-tired stage director. In the half-light of the stage they all seemed shadows, walking or acting in a dream. George, bending to a friend near her in the stall, whispered: "A gathering of lunatics, really. People must be mad to walk those boards."

Bocage, actor, Republican, and former director of the Odéon, became one of her stanchest friends. Mesdames Lambert and Béranger from the Comédie Française came to Nohant regularly. Rachel, then the mistress of Prince Jerome Napoleon, was introduced to George by her lover. And she befriended Madame Arnould-Plessy, another of Jerome's friends, when he broke with her, taking the poor woman under her wing to help her to forget.

On the whole, however, George did not care for the society of women. "I cannot endure woman for long," she wrote in her autobiography. "Not that I think her less intelligent, but she is a restless being and communicates her spirit to me in spite of myself." George preferred to surround herself with men.

Elizabeth Barrett Browning visited her several times in these days of 1852. According to this delicate Victorian lady, George lived in the "abomination of desolation," surrounded by a crowd of men who filled the room with tobacco smoke, spat on the floor, and occasionally knelt before her, expressing their adoration. In Mrs. Browning's eyes they were a "society of the ragged Red diluted with the lower theatrical." On another occasion this visitor found her sitting like a priestess in a circle of eight or nine men, "giving no oracles except with her splendid eyes, sitting at the corner of the fire and warming her feet quietly, in general silence of the most profound deference."

Mrs. Browning's descriptions leave two curiously dissimilar impressions. The first seems familiar, recalling the noisy and ill-mannered young men in Musset's and Chopin's time. The second is different: the persons represented are immobilized as in an old family daguerreotype. In the middle of the picture is Madame Sand—a somewhat heavy-set woman now, dressed in a darkish gown with wide skirts, the bodice buttoned up to her throat. A little white collar relieves the severity of the dress. The nose, Mrs. Browning thought, is of somewhat Jewish character, the chin recedes and the mouth is not good with its white projecting teeth. But there is a great deal of sweetness in her face; she must have been very beautiful once. One wonders about the silence of the group. What have they been talking about before Mrs. Browning came on the scene? Have they been discussing the Absolute, Madame Sand's latest play, or simply the means to help a friend under suspicion across the border into safe exile? Mrs. Browning leaves no clue. She noticed only the melancholy disdain of the hostess: "A noble woman, under the mud, be certain!"

George's stiff, reticent, and always haughty attitude

seems not to have changed even amid the gay, effervescent, and always emotional theatrical crowd. As a matter of fact, nothing seems changed, not even the circle of adoring young men around her. They have always been there—dull or noisy, and always a little inferior. Perhaps they only seemed inferior in contrast to her. True—Chopin and Musset had met her on an equal footing, held their own in her presence. But they too had been younger, and George had seemed more the mother than the mistress.

"Her man is hard to find," Balzac had said. Would she ever find him? She was now almost past the age where the question might still be answered.

CHAPTER THREE

Day to Day

"FOR the past twenty-five years I have lived from day to day; it has never been otherwise, nor is it my own fault; this winter, for instance, I have not been able to buy a warm coat and dress because the accident with *La Presse* has upset my budget. I can very easily deprive myself of things, even necessary ones; but I do not want a soul in the house—not even the cat—to know or feel it." This was written in 1858. At that time her enormous daily output did not even provide her with a coat.

She had always been in financial difficulties. With a large train of dependents—poor relations, political refugees, young artists or politicians in need of a loan—she also provided for the villagers and paid their doctor's and druggist's bills. There had been large household expenses, the extravagances of Maurice and Solange, and at least till '48 a never-ceasing stream of guests. This retinue of admirers, friends, and parasites had resembled an earlier family set-up—the household of the brilliant Mademoiselle de Verrières. But George went beyond mere entertaining. Some of her biographers have calculated that by the end of her life she had given away more than five hundred thousand francs in actual money, the dowries of her children not included.

She continued to write her novels, her articles, her many letters. Writing was as much her life as ever. Once she awakened in the middle of the night asking herself why, after all, she had this love of producing, whether it was mental necessity, or perhaps a good deal habit. Half asleep, she found another answer to these questions. "It is because nothing in our lives arranges itself according to our wishes, while in our stories we are master of our creatures' destiny!"

She had developed a method of mental hygiene which helped her overcome any momentary fatigue. She communicated her method to Maurice, who sometimes made an attempt at writing himself and was now at a standstill over an antediluvian novel. "Go shake yourself a bit, go for a walk, and if it's raining read a scientific book, which will quickly rid you of your mental fatigue. Never begin work in a tired condition."

She herself worked a great deal in the garden now, digging the earth, raking the lawns, cultivating her flowers. Her health improved with daily exercise, her recurrent liver-complaint subsided. But her daily routine was dull and the days followed one another always in the same pattern. Maurice was a great deal in Paris; Solange, since her divorce, was submerged in a life of social turmoil. Occasionally she would come to Nohant, bringing her small daughter Nini, who was George's great joy. George would have liked to keep the child indefinitely with her, but the parents were still disputing over its guardianship. George worried about Solange for many reasons, particularly over money. She gave her daughter an annuity of six thousand francs, yet she had to confess that she did not always know who else was paying for her daughter's clothes.

George worried about Maurice too. He had tried his hand at many professions. One day he wanted to be a painter, the next day he sought employment as an engraver, then again he turned to writing or discovered in himself an aptitude for natural science. He illustrated books and acquired a respectable collection of butterflies and cocoons.

While Maurice amused himself in Paris, went hunting with his father in Guillery, or joined Prince Jerome on his pleasure-yacht in the Mediterranean, George was almost alone in Nohant. The circle of her intimate friends had been much reduced. Planet and Malgache had died; others were still in exile. George had to resign herself to days of solitude and would often have been completely alone had it not been for Manceau, who for years now had been Nohant's most quiet, unobtrusive guest, George's constant companion.

Manceau, engraver and painter by profession, had been a studio friend of Maurice. He had come to Nohant for a few days and stayed a lifetime, as George's secretary and general manager. Kind, obliging, knowing no moods, he was always occupied with some task. He copied George's manuscripts, took care of her correspondence, put order into her household affairs, watched over Maurice's botanical and entomological treasures, dealt with the publishers and newspapers, and found time to attend to his own business, his engraving—which often helped pay George's household expenses.

George, seeing him bent over his work, often wondered at the extent of his loyalty. She had long since taken it for granted, made little attempt to discover the real cause of his humble love for her. She was grateful: she saw to it that Maurice did not get into the habit of treating him like a servant.

Together with Manceau, George bought a tiny bungalow in Gargilesse, an idyllic little village at the junction of the rivers Indre and Creuse. Nohant was often too much of an expense or was suddenly noisy with Maurice's guests, and George needed a refuge of her own. Gargilesse gave her what she always sought: solitude in nature and the peace and charm of a completely simple life. It also allowed her to indulge in her latest hobby—her interest in natural science.

The Second Empire had revived the passion for botany, zoology, and geology which had excited society a hundred years before, and which the Revolution of 1789 had quenched. It occupied its leisure with collecting stones, shells, plants, and stuffed birds. Botany and zoology became a pleasant pastime for all the empty hours that the growing prosperity and a dead political life engendered. France was for the moment filled with charming and eager young women and men who cut up spiders and frogs and breathlessly pored over their intestines with a magnifying glass. Others started ambitious mineral collections or discussed the mysteries of plant fertilization.

"Nobody understood the least bit about it, but everyone expected universal salvation from it," said George. Sharply aware of all trends of the day, she took up the hobby herself and introduced the subject into her novels. Her heroes and heroines were fully conversant with the most difficult aspects of natural history and spent their time admiring shells and rare cocoons.

George's repeated stays in Gargilesse enabled her to

double her literary output. She wrote thirteen novels and several series of articles during the years 1857–62. Her novel *Le Marquis de Villemer* was popular even before she turned it into a play, and *La Daniella* roused such controversy in the press that it recalled her former fighting days.

La Daniella summarized the impressions George had brought back from Italy in 1855. She had undertaken the journey shortly after Nini Clésinger, Solange's small daughter, had died tragically and alone in a Paris boarding-school where she had been placed by her quarreling parents. George had been deeply shocked by this death, for the child's visits had brightened her otherwise dull and uneventful life. Grandmother George had spent hours with little Nini walking in the park, helping her to build grottoes and little gardens. The child had consoled her for the estrangement from her own children.

A few weeks after Nini's death, George left for Italy accompanied by Maurice and Manceau. Her reaction to Rome, its gardens, monuments, and ruins was one of boredom mingled with scorn. It may be that her sensibilities were tuned to the sound, not the sight. The plastic arts, the delight of harmonious contours, meant nothing to her, while the murmur of the wind or the song of a street-beggar caught her fancy at once. In a letter, she made this distinction:

"I love everything which characterizes an environment, the sound of carriage wheels, the din of the Paris streets, the cry of a thousand birds in the country, the movement and noise of ships landing in the dock. I also love complete and absolute silence—in short I love everything around me, no matter where I am; it is my *auditory idiocy*— a new variety, I suppose."

George did not like Rome. She thought it interesting, curious, beautiful, astonishing, but too dead! She found that her own personality became submerged in the dazzling wealth of Roman history. Its imperial dimensions did not fit the scope of her soul. She grew violently individualistic before this historic collection of the new and ancient Rome. Behind the glamour of tradition and grandeur she found the dirt, poverty, indolence, and crass illiteracy of the Italian populace, suffering under the double tyranny of Austria and the Pope. She insisted that the spirit of liberty and nobility was dead in Rome and that nothing was left for an intelligent person to admire. Oh, yes, the stupid, heartless tourists might still say: "What does it matter if the streets are filled with priests and beggars? It is part of the local color, it goes well with the ruins! One is happy here, one admires the stones and forgets humanity." But she refused to admire or even tolerate anything in this "city of Satan, in this brigand's cavern." She wrote to her Italian friend, Calamatta:

"I want to spit on these people who bend their knees before the cardinals. And since at the moment these are the only people we can talk about, let's do so. I should be satisfied indeed if my words would disgust others with contemporary Rome. I should like to accomplish as much for us [the French], but my hands are tied." George, free to attack the Italian clergy, could not do so in France. The French censor prohibited any diatribe against the native Church, for the Catholic Church dominated all channels of French cultural life.

The clergy had helped Louis Napoleon into power for the sole reason that he did away with the anti-clerical Republic. But once the Prince-President was installed, the Church was pleasantly surprised to find in him an active supporter of its interests. He allowed the Jesuits to come back and re-establish their schools. He introduced a law which put three archbishops on the payroll of the Grand Council of Public Instruction. The country witnessed the rapid increase of religious institutions that gradually monopolized public education. No school-teacher was appointed unless he had passed through a clerical school; no politician had a chance unless he was backed by the clergy. And naturally the Church warred against all radical elements in France and "maintained an intense and daily war against the liberal and democratic press."

When *La Daniella* appeared in the journal *La Presse,* George immediately felt the power of the clergy. The editor of *La Presse* received three warnings from the government, threatening suspension if the novel were not withdrawn. In the end the publication of *La Daniella* was discontinued.

George received the news in Nohant. There was nothing much she could do about it—restrict her budget a little further, renounce the winter coat she had planned to buy. For once she felt thoroughly discouraged. Must her toil prove forever useless?

Watching the morning spiders at their delicate tasks, George thought she heard them sing a song of their own:

"One, two! One, two! Back and forth we weave the thread! We spin! Let us hurry with our work! It is dark.

"One, two. Get on with the work! The coming dawn must see our nets spread anew. Someone destroyed our work today, someone ruined our stores, dragged our precious nets in the mire. No matter! Spin, weave! One, two! Back and forth! Work consoles and repairs.

"Weave and spin! Take up the thread, turn back and forth! And you who destroy our daily and nightly labor, you who try to discourage us—go on sweeping, breaking, tearing down! Cause all the ravage you like. One, two, we go on spinning.

"In the dark corners, in loneliness and dust, the gray spider weaves the tissue of her existence. Active, patient, quick, clever—one, two—the poor spider perseveres. They chase, persecute, threaten her. One, two. The poor spider patiently begins over again.

"Tie the thread! Spin, weave until dawn! One, two!"

Barbès wrote her during these days that to him she seemed much like France herself with her triumphs and defeats. George answered him:

"You compare me to France? At any rate I feel very French, for I do not count my falls, wounds, vain hopes, cruel spiritual defeats, but instead rise up again and gather together the threads of my heart which the thorns of the road have torn to pieces, and I carry that bleeding trophy forever toward God."

George, and with her liberal France, had carried a bleeding heart and a torn banner through the whole last decade, while imperial France had been the powerful and brilliant center of the European stage. But the tide was turning. By 1860 the Second Empire began to show signs of fatigue and decline, and before another decade had gone by, the liberals had forgotten their wounds, patched up the old tricolored flag, and were marching to victory once more.

CHAPTER FOUR

Acclaim Again

SIMPSON, in his book on Louis Napoleon, characterized him as an adventurer "with an adventurer's natural detestation of routine, a wanderer's inherent appetite for change." Napoleon III was naturally unsympathetic toward the status quo in Europe, and under the pretext that the principle of self-determination had to be established set out to change it.

Because of his chauvinism and his restlessness he brought more courage than wisdom to the task. But he was not unlucky at first. At the beginning of the century "the shackles of European routine and order were greatly loosened, and much that was formerly impossible was possible now. With a crowned adventurer in Paris, adventurers in European politics were tolerated," Simpson wrote.

But French foreign policy in the 60's turned the tide against the Emperor. He alienated England and made of the Pope his bitterest foe. Worse, Napoleon's main factional support in France—the monarchists and the Catho-

lic clergy—turned against him on account of his awkward
Italian policy.

Napoleon with his love for dramatics did something very
surprising in answer to the rising tide of opposition, domestic and foreign. He turned liberal. During the 60's
the fetters that had tied the press and the legislative bodies
were slowly loosened. In a little while he gave the Chamber
the right to question the ministers on their policies and
acts. Sharp supervision of the polls was relaxed. Also a
commercial treaty with England was signed, which instituted what amounted to free trade between the two countries.

But the new liberalism weakened the Emperor's prestige. To counteract the bad impression, he undertook more
crusades: to Syria, into the Far East, and more notably into
Mexico, where the French had backed the accession of the
unfortunate Maximilian. But while, in the decade before,
every adventure of Louis Napoleon had been a success, now
everything he touched turned into ashes.

George said: "Today there are three dozen kinds of
weather in the political world. Take our Emperor, for instance, who abandons his darling little Pope, takes England to his heart again, and after having invited all Europe
to lunch, tells them the soup is spilled and they had better
stay at home. It seems to me that all these improvisations
are much too bizarre to deserve admiration. If at the beginning of the quarrel there had been courage and frankness, war could have been avoided. A government with
principles and a more stable attitude does not need so much
blood and money to make itself respected. The prestige of
this ruler is sustained by his surprise politics. That may
have its amusing points, but it is less strong than it looks."

She remained relatively indifferent to the political happenings of the day. She continued writing books and plays which were mostly without thesis or dogma. On the whole the 60's augured better for Madame Sand than for Louis Napoleon.

Maurice had married Lina Calamatta, daughter of George's old engraver friend Luigi Calamatta. The young couple had settled in Nohant and before long George realized that she had found in Lina a devoted daughter. Lina told her friends: "I married George Sand rather than Maurice Sand; I married him because I adored her."

The couple had been married by the civil authorities and later by a Protestant minister. Neither George nor Maurice wanted a Catholic marriage, yet in order to assure Maurice's children a Christian education some compromise had to be found. George had corresponded with several Protestant ministers in the country and tested their tolerance and dogma before making her choice. Had they any Popish inclinations? Did they believe in the divinity of Christ? Did they believe in the dogma of hell? The latter point disquieted George particularly.

"Jesus believes in hell and likes to believe in it. His religion of tenderness and mercy is good enough for humanity, but not good enough for God Himself. He hopes that his Father will avenge him; he hopes that the virtues of his disciples will heap burning coals on the heads of his persecutors and condemn them to the fiery Gehenna. . . . Either Jesus never said so, or he is not God."

George was much interested in Renan's *Life of Christ*, published about this time, but she did not agree with all of Renan's points. "Jesus is not and cannot be the last word of truth accorded to mankind," she wrote to a friend. "You tell me somewhat ambiguously that he has preached a progressive truth capable of development. But did he know this? I don't think so. He was a man of his time, although the most idealistic one. Remark the doubtful attitude of this founder of Christianity! It opens the door wide for many contradictions. His beautiful doctrine has resulted in evil as well as in good simply because its source is a myth. It is a beautiful ray of light, but its sun is hidden in the clouds. Plato, Pythagoras, and other founders of better-defined doctrines have brought only good to mankind. Jesus has brought hypocrisy and persecution to society for 1800 years or so. This very moment we are still persecuted in his name, deprived of liberty and harassed by priests. Therefore get thee hence, God Jesus! We shall love thee as a philosopher—thou charming figure from an oriental story-book."

George was still warring against the tyranny of the Church; in fact, her excitement seemed to increase year after year. In 1863 she came out in an open attack on French Catholicism in her novel, *Mademoiselle La Quintinie*. The book was a sharp denunciation of Jesuit practices and influences in French family life. For the first time in fifteen years George dared to resume the militant attitude of her former *romans à thèse*.

The story roused a good deal of excitement. As in the days of *Lélia* the readers were split into two camps: those who applauded her with enthusiasm, those who were horrified by her atheism. But the publicity was useful and much needed, too, for it recalled George Sand to a public that had almost forgotten her. But if her return to popularity was not immediately apparent, it was made certain by *Le Marquis de Villemer*, produced in Paris the following year. The play was a literary triumph. And mingled with the applause for its literary qualities were respect and enthusiasm for the author of *Mademoiselle La Quintinie*.

George had expected a certain amount of agitation on the opening night of her play. She never expected the uproar and commotion it actually caused. The audience was beside itself, applauding frantically after each scene, sometimes after each phrase. The whole Latin Quarter had gathered to support it against any possible intrigues of the clerics. Outside the theater two cavalry regiments were ready for action. The theater was filled with high officials and foreign diplomats. The imperial couple was present and of course George's friend Jerome Bonaparte, "the red prince." Before the play was over, Napoleon III had shed tears of emotion, and Jerome had ruined his gloves from too much applauding.

Outside, the crowd was waiting for George's appearance, and when she came greeted her with shouts of "Long live George Sand! Long live *Mademoiselle La Quintinie!* Down with the Jesuits!"

After the second performance George wrote to her son in Nohant: "There was some noise again on the square tonight, just a slight inclination to repeat the performance of last night which assumed much greater proportions than I expected. Six thousand people are said to have rushed to the Catholic Club and the House of the Jesuits, singing and caterwauling: 'Holy Spirit descend upon us' and other chants. It really was not very wicked, but as all these children had become intoxicated partly from shouting so much, partly from having waited twelve hours in line before the play opened, the police feared a disturbance and dispersed them. Nobody was beaten or wounded, though. The authorities had expected worse upheavals and two regiments have been in readiness. The students had planned to unharness my horses and lead me home in triumph; fortunately they were prevented from doing so. Some sang the

'Sire de Framboisy' to tease the Empress, but the Emperor behaved very well; he applauded the play and afterwards walked to his carriage, since the coachman could not drive up with the crowds blocking the entrance. But the Emperor refused to have the way cleared for him and the people appreciated it and applauded him."

George's family was particularly pleased as the Odéon was sold out night after night. The box-office receipts soared to 5000 francs a day. They might have averaged more, but George wrote to her children apologetically: "The schools, the workmen, the liberal thinkers, and those friends who from personal sympathy will advertise the play get passes, and that seems to me a good and honest policy!" Enough was left to replenish the home treasury.

Two months after her glorious success she returned to Nohant, not to stay but to pack her trunks and depart for a long absence. She had bought a small house at Palaiseau, in the vicinity of Paris, for herself and Manceau, while Lina and Maurice were to remain in charge of Nohant. George told her friends that she expected the young couple to become more self-reliant through this change; Palaiseau on the other hand would allow her to supervise her theatrical productions more closely. It was not so. In Nohant the same situation existed as in Chopin's time: Maurice now objected to the presence of Manceau and was jealous of his influence over his mother. But this time George did not yield to her son's ultimatum. Maurice no longer needed her; he was settled with a wife and a home. It was Manceau who deserved her solicitude. He had sacrificed years of his life to her, and he was a very sick man.

The public gossiped about the decision; George's Berry friends were shocked. The villagers were perturbed that the kind mistress of Nohant was abandoning them. The workmen from La Châtre sent a letter begging George to stay. The letter began with "Dear and famous compatriot," spoke of her genius that filled the world with light, and her words that knew how to touch the hearts of the simple people. It praised her kindness, her democratic attitude, her wonderful appreciation of the toil and dignity of the laboring classes. It spoke with respect of *The Journeyman-Joiner* and applauded *Mademoiselle La Quintinie*. It closed with a song from *Consuelo* and praised George as the Goddess of the Poor. Madame Sand could ask for no better and finer appreciation from her countrymen anywhere.

Nevertheless her decision was final. Maurice and Lina took their mother and Manceau to the station in Châteauroux.

George, traveling north to Orléans that day, may have remembered that once before she had left Nohant "for good." At that time it was winter and the moon shone over frozen swamps. Bare black trees lined the highways, swaying a little in the night wind, recalling the ghosts of an earlier epoch. The carriage had been cold.

Now there was no carriage: George could travel by train. And it was June and daytime. The landscape had changed a good deal since she had taken her first trip to Paris as a child. The huge forests, particularly farther north near Orléans where bandits had roamed in her grandmother's youth, had considerably thinned or disappeared. Cities had grown and so had villages. Many a chimney-stack rose from small valleys where formerly had been but an occasional windmill. Roads had grown straighter and wider. George could not help thinking that an invisible Casimir might have had a hand in correcting them.

George had passed through these plains and river valleys so many times that she could not remember when the changes had first taken place. Nor did she recall the thoughts, emotions, and images that had flashed through her mind on her former trips. "We live in the present only," she told herself with a sigh. Here and there a small forgotten valley, the outline of a hill, or the sight of a picturesque hut would awaken a brief nostalgia which she was at a loss to explain.

She smiled at Manceau sitting opposite her, busy with some accounts he had left undone and which he hoped to finish while the train jerked slowly on. Manceau was always active and at the same time kept a kind, considerate, cheerful attitude. Sometimes she felt remorse that she gave him so little in return. But then—he was not one of those weak souls who eternally claim happiness from others without giving it themselves; he was strong through his own abundant generosity and expected little in exchange.

They felt quickly at home at Palaiseau. The house was tiny but comfortable and they seemed to have been particularly happy in the choice of their servants. The country around, with its rolling hills, green meadows, orchards, brooks, and small woods, was harmonious and pleasant. The small village itself offered little diversion and was dead after six o'clock at night. "Even on Sundays there are very few Parisians about—no *flâneurs*, very few bourgeois." The roads were excellent and in the evening after dinner George and Manceau would walk at least two miles.

There were no wild rides and hunting trips now. George, wearing a hat and gloves, promenaded on a village road in mid-Victorian manner, accompanied by a well-behaved gentleman who discoursed with her in quiet tones. Occasionally they would stop for conversation with an elderly neighbor who loved to fish in the brooklet near their house. The meadow, covered with white, yellow, and purple flowers, offered seats in the form of huge blocks of granite left there from the glacial age. The Victorian lady and her escort would sit down and converse a while on the size of this year's trout or the botanical variety of the place, for instance the local wild orchid.

Sometimes George would walk a little farther by herself and find a picturesque field where she cared to linger. An angry peasant would come running to chase her away, but on recognizing her would politely lift his cap and say: "Oh, it's you, Madame Sand! Now don't you go away! Rest here as long as you want to. Don't tire yourself out."

The natives, rather well-to-do peasants, were agreeable and helpful. They provided the household with vegetables and fruit.

The house itself was the last one on leaving the village. It had a little garden. Day and night the calm of the place was absolute. George, accustomed to long vigils, sat by the window at night, listening to the silence and its thousand mysterious voices. It seemed to her that she was gaining a new understanding of the cosmos and all things in it, that her individuality acquired a new sense of relationship to the universe. She tried to explain it to Manceau: "I cannot command this mood, but there are hours when I seem to get outside myself, when I live in a plant or a cloud, when I become bird, tree-top, flowing water, horizon, color, form, or changing sensation! There are hours when I circle with the swallows or roam with the lizards, when I fly, swim, drink dew. We are no abstract beings, my friend. Heaven and earth act on us at all moments and we feed on everything in our environment: air, heat, humidity, electricity, and the vitality of our fellow-men. Everything which is outside us is also within us. The 'non-I' does not exist, nor does the 'I' . . . at least not in an absolute sense."

Manceau chided her for sitting beside the open window so long without a shawl on her shoulders. He listened a little impatiently when she explained her "mute contemplations," as he called them. He did not understand what she talked about and after a while left her to herself again. George did not mind. She was accustomed to preach to deaf ears, particularly when she tried to formulate her more mystical moods. Musset, Chopin, they all had been ironical on that point. Liszt alone had seconded her.

But she was happy in her present atmosphere. Long enthusiastic reports about her new life were sent to distant friends. Her books were composed in pleasant, almost Vergilian mood. She told herself: "Here happiness has finally caught up with me! It is an unexpected happiness with an unknown face. As a skeptic and seeker for truth I must question, analyze, and weigh this newcomer. Yes, friend happiness, let me look at you, but don't come too close! I know you are inconstant and a creature of this world; you cannot really offer me paradise. If I lingered too long with you I might find you only a fantasy, a state of mind, a creation of my momentary thoughts, a passing emotion, a fragrance in the wind."

After he had been six months in Palaiseau Manceau's tuberculosis became acute. Cough and fever grew worse. Doctors were consulted, new treatments tried. Sometimes they offered a short relief and George would be immediately more hopeful about her friend's condition. But from May 1865 on she realized that he was doomed. Again her nights and days were spent by the bedside of a suffering friend, again she passed through all the stages of concern, pity, fear, and despair. But she did not abandon Manceau as she had abandoned Chopin. She nursed him to the last. He died in her arms early one morning in August.

His death left the house melancholy and empty. George went restlessly from one room to another, trying to conquer her fatigue, her grief, her loneliness. Nothing spoke in those silent rooms but the voice of a shade. Yes, Manceau's shade was there still, not an unhappy shade, but it seemed to complain that it could no longer talk to her, share her work and responsibilities.

The nursing had been long and difficult and George was broken with fatigue. She had not left the house for weeks, spending night after night on a couch near the dying man. But helpful friends had come to see her during that last trying period and an uninterrupted round of duties had prevented her from yielding to dejection. Now that she had time, insomnia kept her from recuperating. She tried to work. Why work? The voice of happiness within her was dead. Silence outside and within her.

The death of her friend had left her hands idle and her soul drained. She realized now what he had meant to her life. He had built a wall of protection and love around her, had given her the warmth of his heart. He had given her what she had vainly sought in her former friendships: emotional stability. Perhaps it had come too late in life to be of deep significance to her, but when it was gone she wanted it back.

For a time life seemed not to be worth while continuing. She told Flaubert: "It is easy to be courageous during the battle. But afterward, when all is over, one's duty done, condolences accepted, the tender concern of our loved ones satisfied—when one starts anew on one's road to work and life, what then? The real grief begins when the struggle is over. One seems to live again, but in what darkness and solitude! Are we simply worn out by our tears and despair, or has life diminished within us? I find it difficult to believe that we keep our soul intact when we lose the ones we love."

Maurice Sand came to take her home to Nohant. She was glad to see him; it gave her a release into a stream of tears. But she could not go to Nohant now.

"Not yet," she told her son. She wanted to live with her memories a little longer. She was reluctant to leave the house that had sheltered her last friendship and retained the image of the man who had been the last link in her long chain of emotional experiences. Going back to Nohant meant that old age had come.

CHAPTER FIVE

The Friend Flaubert

THE brothers Goncourt, then rising to fame with the new naturalist school, report in their diary an interview with Madame Sand in 1862. They visited her at her Paris apartment. Manceau opened the door and led them into Madame Sand's presence.

"We entered a very large hall, very much like a studio. Seated at the window, with her back toward us, was a gray shadow, a woman who remained motionless and was apparently unaware of our bow and our greeting. This shadow, which seemed asleep, was Madame Sand. . . . She gives the impression of an automaton; she speaks with utter monotony, as it were mechanically; her voice is dull and without cadence. Her attitude is serious and quiet and recalls the sleepy calm of ruminating cattle. Her gestures are slow, circumspect, like those of a sleep-walker. With methodical precision she lights one match after another and holds it to her cigarette; thus we see her face."

Their conversation was difficult. The brothers found her

sayings so trite and naïve that they made them "shiver." In the end they were glad to take their leave.

The description was characteristic enough as far as George's attitude toward her interviewers was concerned. She was very conscious of her awkward conversational manner. Years before, when Sainte-Beuve had announced his intention of visiting her, she had written to him: "You will find me stupid."

To the brothers Goncourt she seemed more than unintelligent. She was the ossified past, something that the life current had long since pushed toward the more quiet waters of the river banks. The Goncourts felt themselves to be in the midstream of life. They were urbane, metropolitan; they were inhabitants of the most amusing, fashionable, modern city of the world. They were Parisians of the 60's.

Paris was then the brilliant center of Europe, where the nations gave themselves rendezvous, where a lovely empress in crinoline skirts set the fashion of the day, where people danced to the waltzes of Offenbach, where the opera ballets were staged in the most dazzling gas-light, where people had money, ideas, and lived at a breathless pace. And the frame was equally brilliant, for Paris had been rebuilt in true dictator style. Streets had been broadened, old quarters torn down, new roads built between the south and the north, the west and the east. The Etoile began to radiate triumphant avenues in every direction; squares and parks were laid out in the English fashion. The Parisians had sewers now; the inner city had begun to encroach upon the suburbs.

The Goncourts were children of this new era and they felt they spoke its language. It was a different language from that of Madame Sand. The Goncourts did not understand her when she spoke of liberty and the glory of France,

the nobility and the grandeur of the revolutionary concepts.
Her phrases smacked of 1830, no, of the century of Rousseau. They themselves were adverse to her declamatory republicanism. Their own language was sharp and to the
point, their minds scientific and matter of fact. Theirs was
the vision of the scientist who is accustomed to study the
part rather than the whole; who sees life through a micro-
scope and disregards the cosmos which George's generation
had so lovingly embraced. George in the present world was
a Romantic lost among the Realists.

But the Goncourts misjudged the situation and exaggerated it in their own favor. George was not yet a monument
of the past. Two years later the success of both *Le Marquis
de Villemer* and *Mademoiselle La Quintinie* proved her
to be still an important public figure. Her anti-clerical novel
in particular had gained for her the respect and attention
even of the younger literary generation, for her style was
realistic and the action tense. Everybody wanted her to
adapt the novel to the stage; when it was done the government prohibited the performance, though it had not prohibited the publication of the novel. The play was not produced, either then or under the Third Republic. Thiers, too,
refused to give offense to the clerics.

George was back in the literary current. The producers
were eager for her plays and Buloz, with whom she had become reconciled after years of disagreement, published her
novels again in the *Revue*. Another friend and adviser had
been won back—Sainte-Beuve. And there was always imperial benediction in the background. The Emperor and his
wife were known to read all of Sand's books and made it a
point to appear at every one of her premieres.

Louis Napoleon had never outgrown his early admiration for the author of *Indiana*, with whom he had discussed,

if only in writing, his first socialist essay, "On the Extinction of Pauperism." He would have liked her to be a member of the French Academy or winner of the Prix Gobert—a prize of 20,000 francs. He and the Empress were disappointed when the prize went to Thiers instead, and would gladly have offered Madame Sand a private donation if she would have accepted it. But George had her Republican principles. She could only accept the Empress's donation when funds for some charity were needed. She let her contribute to the education of Dorval's children.

George was a friendly enemy of the imperial house. Her Republican friends thought her much too friendly and avoided her for that reason. They called her a secret Bonapartist and pointed to her autobiography in support. She had once called its first part: "The History of a Family, from Fontenoy to Marengo," and it culminated in a distinct glorification of the name and deeds of Bonaparte. The book was the best bit of propaganda Napoleon III had had during his reign and before. No wonder he applauded at Madame Sand's first-night performances.

George could not understand her friends' irritation. She had never glorified the new house of Bonaparte, but had erected a monument to Napoleon I, who, as a real Republican in his reforms and policies, had ultimately attempted to strengthen the ideals of the great French Revolution. She had never committed herself in favor of the present Emperor, but rather against him. It was not her fault that he had become ruler in France, but that of the French masses who had once voted him into power. France had wanted him, for whatever obscure reasons. France would get rid of him when the time came. She had often told her friends: "Men rise to power one day and are overthrown the next. . . . These are the minor mishaps in the history of democracy. History from now on will not so much record the deeds and gestures of certain men as study the aspirations, reactions, and manifestations of the masses."

After 1863 George took part in the famous Magny dinners where the Goncourts, Maupassant, Zola, Flaubert, Taine, Renan, Gautier, Berthelot the chemist, and other prominent men met for informal discussions. George did not feel at home among so many brilliant minds. Gautier's dazzling paradoxes confused her, the cutting criticism of the brothers Goncourt took her breath away. Berthelot seemed too important to be bothered with naïve questions on chemistry. She whispered into Flaubert's ear: "You are the only one here who does not frighten me."

Most of the men in these gatherings felt toward her as the Goncourts did. They were amazed at her old-fashioned idealism. They considered her belief in the progress of humanity a superstition; Maupassant disrespectfully called her "eighteenth century." Even Taine had difficulties in seeing her as a contemporary, but because he was fond of her he likened her to Goethe, pointing out that her life and work, like his, made an ideal pattern. Renan was the most generous among them. "My God," he said, "I think Madame Sand is greater than Balzac! She will still be read three hundred years from now."

George was the oldest among them and it was inevitable that the younger writers should feel removed from her. George herself was aware of the situation. She realized that their ideology differed from hers by a century, and she formulated this realization in her own way when she wrote to Barbès:

"We are forced to pass through an era of darkness, where our memories—those of the glorious Revolution and the

great days that left our spirit aflame—will disappear with
the rest. But does it matter? . . . Something within us remains eternally alive and will help to resuscitate a more
idealistic humanity. The moral atheism of today was inevitable and the result of an exaggerated mystical development. Man, deceived and misguided during so many centuries, now hopes to find salvation in the experimental
method. Once he has experimented enough, he will see that
this is not yet the answer. The France which is under an
eclipse now will then once more become the France of
miracles."

It was at the Magny dinners that George had first met
the man who thereafter became the center of her friendship and literary interest: Flaubert. She had known him
since 1863 and he proved a particularly helpful friend in
the years after Manceau's death. He had come to Palaiseau
to brighten her solitude a little; he invited her to Croisset,
where he lived with his mother and niece. Gustave Flaubert was forty-five and George sixty-two, but she did not
call him "my son" as she was wont to do with the younger
Dumas. Theirs was a bachelor companionship based on mutual artistic respect and understanding, though Flaubert
called himself George's disciple. She realized the importance
of his work, which had not yet found full recognition, and
was convinced that Flaubert's genius was greater than her
own.

Their correspondence is as valuable as any document
written with an eye on posterity. It is carefully phrased,
filled with topics of general interest, but not very spontane-
ous and not very personal. Perhaps this was Flaubert's fault;
he remained icily aloof and objective even in the face of an
occasional personal remark. He never revealed himself,
though George with feminine curiosity tried to break the

GUSTAVE FLAUBERT
Painting by Giraud *(Musée de Versailles)*

hard shell, dig under the correct and conventional surface
to find some weakness, some human response, some personal characteristic of "the troubadour," as she called him.
"You are rather a special being," she told him, "mysterious, though gentle as a lamb. I have been very eager to
question you, but my very great respect has hindered me
from doing so, for I can only deal with my own disasters;
those of a great mind which must have suffered much to
get into a producing state like yours are too sacred to be
touched upon brutally or lightly. Sainte-Beuve, who likes
you, tells me nevertheless that you are terribly vicious. . . .
I suppose a man of intelligence can have a great deal of
curiosity. I never had it myself, I was not courageous
enough. I have preferred to leave my mind incomplete; that
is my own affair, and anyone is free to embark on a big
ship with sails flying, or a small fishing-boat. The artist is
an explorer who must not be stopped by anything and who
is neither right nor wrong if he goes to the right or the left.
His goal justifies everything."

Or again:

"How is the novel getting on? Your courage has not yet
failed you? Your solitude does not weigh you down? I am
sure it is not very complete, and somewhere there is a lovely
friend who comes and goes or lives near by. But you are a
recluse nevertheless. I myself am too much alone with the
dead in Palaiseau, not enough alone when I go to Nohant."

Sometimes her maternal feelings came to the fore and
she chided him for his exaggerated seclusion. She urged
him humorously to get out of his slippers and dressing-
gown and take a walk. "Walk up to the little vineyard behind your house every day at noon. Do it for my sake."
She had much astute advice on the hygiene of a person confined all day to his desk. She insisted that the routine must

be broken by a certain amount of physical exercise or the nervous system would suffer.

In 1866 she visited Flaubert in his home near Rouen. She met his mother and niece; inspected his home, his garden, the environs; observed his ascetic habits. She saw the Seine, flat, calm, and yellow, as it passed under his window; she heard the shrieking of the iron chain at the landing below—a sound which tortured Flaubert's delicate nerves.

She enjoyed her visit to Croisset immensely, because she could talk about the things nearest to her heart. "It is wonderful to be able to talk about one's life. Anyway, these things are much less complicated than the bourgeois suspects, and the mysteries we reveal to a friend are just the opposite of what a stranger supposes them to be."

She was much touched watching Flaubert in the midst of his family, and praised him for his gentleness and kindness. That he called his mother "my daughter" brought tears to her eyes. But she saw him essentially as an artist. In consequence she liked to discuss the artist's personality with him. "The artist's soul is full of subtle reactions and rich in quiet and attentive curiosities. . . . You will also find that any real artist is fearful of himself, for he cannot surrender without incurring the danger of annihilation and because a deep purity prevents him from spending and wasting the treasures of his soul."

She confessed that she had planned a novel on the artist (the real one) but that she felt unworthy to go ahead with it. She was not the perfect artist herself, she told Flaubert; in fact she had a touch of the *épicier* in her soul—she loved to calculate, classify, teach, sew, and scrub the children. Nor was she too fond of perfection in any form.

One of the subjects that caused a prolonged controversy between them was that of the artist's chastity. Is it wise for the artist to let himself go in reckless pursuit of passionate sensation or should he abstain altogether? Flaubert thought that work and pleasure each had their time. But George objected. The great artist—the man "who knows that pleasure can be immense as the infinite and that work is passionate enthusiasm"—cannot deal with either art or love by way of routine. Also nature has placed its limitations on human capacity. The great artists were seldom potent or else had exhausted their virility at an early date. The Don Juans were no Byrons and the Byrons no Don Juans. Don Juan did not write poetry, and Byron was said to be an unsatisfactory lover.

"He [Byron] must of course have known the ecstasy of heart, brain, and senses; he must have known enough of them or he could not have written his love poems. We do not need much to set our hearts a-flutter; but we would be ruined by the storm of eternal small appetites. . . . All excess of work kills and so does all excess of pleasure. But the greater the personality the more it will exceed the bounds of ordinary powers.

"No," George concluded, "I have no definite theories in this matter. As usual, I ask questions and wait for others to answer."

During the years before the Franco-Prussian War her life was relatively restless. By 1867 her residence was again Nohant, though she hardly stayed there, traveling extensively: to Paris, Croisset, Palaiseau, Brittany, and Provence. Her health made her prefer a warmer climate in winter now and she usually went to the Riviera for a month or two after Christmas. Her vitality was greatly impaired by recurrent intestinal attacks—the result of typhoid fever she had contracted in 1860.

Maurice now managed many of her personal affairs, and George stated with satisfaction that life had finally given her the freedom and leisure she had longed for over so many years.

In 1866 she had dedicated her novel *Last Love* to Flaubert; while preparing a new book at Nohant the following year, she wrote to him that she had been a prisoner too long to find her liberty without flaw. "I am well, I work, I am finishing *Cadio*. The weather is warm, I live, I am calm and sad, and don't know why. The sweet gentle life I lead demoralizes my soul, though it strengthens my physique. I suffer from a kind of spleen which is all roses and honey but a spleen nevertheless."

Cadio is the story of a peasant of the great Revolution, showing the effects of great historical happenings on the man in the street—how, under the pressure of important events, a simple unpolitical person will reveal unsuspected heights or depths of character and act accordingly. In her preface to *Cadio* she cited an instance known to her from the Revolution of 1848, which proved her point. But the press accused her of using the incident to rouse ancient hatreds which had better be forgotten. George denied this. She maintained that the contemplation of cruelty in the historical past did not cause the spectator to wish for more or for revenge, but made him insist rather that all future struggle be prohibited and peace enforced at any price. Yet, as this "peace at any price" was another delusion, she maintained, and led only to the display of more force and brutality, a different solution must be sought. Let the public be enlightened, let historical events and data be discussed in all their aspects, so that mankind may learn to deal with future catastrophes. But let not indifference or cowardice cover up historical crime.

Late in 1869 she lost her good friend Sainte-Beuve. George had gone to his funeral with many other notables and prominent men of letters. The crowd pressed around them, curious to see their faces, to whisper and to comment. But when George returned from the graveside, this same crowd ostentatiously formed a passage to let her through in silence, the men with their heads uncovered. George was deeply touched.

In February 1870 her play *L'Autre* was produced at the Odéon with Sarah Bernhardt in the leading role. *L'Autre* was as triumphant a success as *Le Marquis de Villemer* had been. She had written it without collaboration. The box-office receipts soared to new heights and George wrote to her children on March 2: "I shall be home Saturday by the usual train. I am overjoyed to be back with you soon and with such wonderful news."

Less than half a year later the war broke out between France and Prussia over the accession of a Hohenzollern prince to the Spanish throne.

CHAPTER SIX

War, Without and Within

NAPOLEON III did not want the war; neither his health nor his courage was any longer equal to the task. But Bismarck had played his cards well, and before long France was involved not only with Prussia but with the South German states.

France, however, was sure of its ultimate victory. Its chauvinistic frenzy ran high, as if it were feeding on the repressions of the last twenty years. Chauvinism in France had never been the prerogative of but a single conservative or nationalistic group; it was also a part of French liberal politics. Rousseau long before had declared the Rhine, the sea, the Alps, and the Pyrenees to be the national frontiers of his country. The men of the great Revolution took up his dream. In 1794 Merlin de Thionville proclaimed: "The Republic must dictate the laws of Europe."

Napoleon I, in fighting his wars of aggrandizement, lived up to this "mysticism of conquest" and gave it food for another hundred years. Nor did the nation lose hold of its chauvinistic ideals under the next regime, when its foreign prestige was again at a low ebb. In 1822 Chateaubriand still hoped "that a well-conducted Republic might dictate those laws Thionville has spoken of." The Bourbons were apparently not capable of it; neither were the Orléans. Louis-Philippe refrained from going after hypothetical laurels; he did not believe in embroiling the nation in any military adventure, and this unwonted pacifism, rather than lack of reform, cost him his throne.

Napoleon III had at first satisfied the country's desire for glory, but in the 60's his foreign policy had become less glorious and he rapidly lost in popularity. But was this France really so militant, or was it mainly vainglorious? Guizot had said: "I believe a nation is capable of revolutionary violence; I do not believe in its permanent revolutionary instincts."

A factor which keyed the nation's patriotism to a new pitch appeared: the rise of Prussia to leadership among the Germanic states and its ever-growing ambition to expand.

Guizot had been struck by the possibility of the formation of a greater Germany as early as 1847 when the Prussian king gave his country a constitution. "An ambitious Prussia might from now on turn the following ideas to its advantage—ideas which it seems to have appropriated already—Germanic unity and the liberal spirit. With the help of these two levers it could slowly undermine the secondary Germanic states, attract, enchain, incorporate them, to the effect that the actual Germanic status would be profoundly changed and that of Europe in its wake."

In 1870 Guizot's prediction seemed to come true. Bismarck had shuffled the cards in order to draw his big trump: Prussian supremacy within the Germanic states. This meant an open threat to the status quo in Europe and more

immediately to the assumed supremacy of the French nation. Napoleon III could no more turn the impulses of his
countrymen into peaceful channels now than try to stop a
stampeding herd.

When the war broke out, George was in Nohant. Drought,
disorder, and fear owing to the lack of communication, had
demoralized the country almost at once, even before the
disastrous bulletins from the battlefields arrived. George
wrote in her diary: "The general hatred and fury, and the
consternation concerning the government, are unbelievable.
The frightful disorder causes mistrust everywhere."

Though Berry was actually far removed from the
front, troops were stationed everywhere. Ill-equipped, ill-
provisioned, they begged and stole while waiting for transportation to the battlefields. The lack of preparedness was
evident. Youths under conscription practiced in the village
squares with a few hunting guns and many wooden sticks.
By September 1 Sedan was lost, the Emperor made a prisoner, and Paris had set up the Republic with Thiers and
Trochu as its heads. Very soon Paris was encircled by the
enemy troops. News from her friends reached George by
balloon only. In November the troops were swarming back
from the front in rags. La Châtre had a small-pox epidemic. While the siege of Paris was under way, George remained in Nohant, ready to help her neighbors and friends.
Her general reaction to the frightful catastrophe of the war
found expression in her *Journal of a Traveler during the
War*, and in a series of articles published in the *Revue*. Her
tone, at first calm and conciliatory, became bitter, almost
shrill, against the enemy.

George had greeted the return of the Republic with joy
and hope for the future. She felt that the Republic and universal franchise still were the panacea for all ills.

"Universal suffrage has its rights today and tomorrow, even if we should have more dictatorships or alternately constitutional and absolutist governments. . . . Learn to judge things from a higher level. Then nothing frightens, nothing fascinates in the immediate future. We feel that we must endure and march on, and march on and endure, and the one reassuring fact is that it is impossible to stop going on, that movement is life itself."

These lines had been written as early as 1863 as part of a letter on "Equality" addressed to Edouard Rodrigues. She reiterated her democratic credo when in March 1871 the Commune was established in Paris in opposition to Thiers. She still believed in universal suffrage and the rights of the people but she repulsed the all-too-radical Commune. She faced this new social experiment with the bitterness of a disappointed revolutionary whose ideals have been badly misinterpreted. Her scorn of the new revolutionary government of Paris was summed up in the following points:

"The Commune objects to the power arising from universal suffrage and yet avails itself of that suffrage for its own constitution.

"It has discarded the appearance of legality which it tried to assume, and acts by brute force without seeking any other claim than that of hatred and contempt for everything that is not part of itself.

"It proclaims practical social science, declaring itself its sole depositary, but it does not make mention of it in its decisions and decrees.

"It declares that it has come to deliver man from his fetters and prejudices, and immediately sets up absolute power and threatens with death whosoever is not convinced of its infallibility.

"It usurps social papacy and imitates the dictatorships.

"What kind of Republic is that? I see nothing vital or rational, nothing constitutional."

The members of the Commune were either followers of the communist Blanqui or of the syndicalist Proudhon. Engels said that only a small minority knew of the principles of German scientific socialism as formulated by Marx and himself. The Commune advocated the association of free and independent municipalities whose representatives were to be chosen by universal vote, but not from the bourgeois classes. It was, as Marx said, not a parliamentary but a working body with executive and legislative power. This regime was to spread all over France, replacing the older form of centralized government.

It was evident that Proudhon had converted the Paris Commune to the principles he had already preached in the 40's: those of absolute equality of condition, of fortune, and of salary. At that time the police had declared that his ideas were dangerous indeed but that fortunately nobody paid any attention to them. He had no following among the artists and intellectuals of the pre-revolutionary decade; they disliked him heartily, for he had declared talent a deformity of character which would cease to exist with the establishment of full equality. Proudhon wanted neither competition nor superior minds; he did not even want a government, for he was essentially anarchic. Any hierarchy was odious to him.

While George ostentatiously sided against the Commune, her former fellow-revolutionaries like Blanc and other exiles fluttered back to Paris in the hope of participating in the glory of the new revolutionary regime. But the Commune had no interest in their efforts at co-operation. The leaders of the proletarian government called them old-fashioned and unscientific and would have nothing to do with them. Proudhon's syndicalism ruled the day.

George in the meantime stood on the side of Thiers and the legal government in Versailles. She praised Thiers for his strength of character during the crisis and because "he adopted the Republican form of government contrary to his personal feelings." She was pleased when he proved victorious in the struggle with the Commune and showed herself overjoyed "that the orgy of pretended renovators" had come to an end.

"Unfortunate International! Is it true that you believe in the lie of might over right? If you are as powerful and as numerous as you are supposed to be, is it possible that you profess destruction and hatred as a duty?"

She had traveled far since the days of her proclamation in 1848 when she spoke like a mother to the people of France—the kind, gentle people. Worlds separated the members of the Commune from the socialist veteran of 1848.

But George's heart bled over the country's general disaster. Flaubert could declare with Olympian calm that the masses were always stupid and the world had to be hated, but George answered with vehemence:

"Do you want me to give up loving? Do you want me to say that I have deceived myself all my life, that humanity is contemptible, hateful, and was and will be? And you reproach me for my grief, as if it were a childish regret for a lost illusion? You tell me that the public has always been savage, the priest hypocritical, the bourgeois cowardly, the soldier a brigand, and the peasant stupid? You tell me that you have known this since you were young and that your maturity has taught you nothing else? Then you have never been young. Ah, we are very different indeed, for I have never ceased to be young, if to be young means to love."

No, she could not sleep peacefully while the earth trembled beneath her. "We cannot isolate ourselves, we cannot break the intimate ties which bind us to our next of kin; we cannot curse or despise our own species. Humanity is not an empty word. Our life is made of love, and not to love means not to live. You say: the people! But you and I are this people. . . . There are no two races; all differences and class distinctions are relative or even illusory."

So far as victorious Germany was concerned, she could not but prophesy its ultimate downfall in consequence of its present impudent pride. "The German nation will be as much an object of pity for its victories as we are for our defeats, for they are the first step toward her moral dissolution. The drama of her overthrow has commenced, and as she is working at it with her own hands, it will make rapid progress. All great material organizations where right, justice, and respect for humanity are disregarded are objects of clay.

"Well, the moral degradation of Germany is not the future salvation of France; its destruction would not restore us to life. It is not by blood that nations renew their strength and become rejuvenated. The breath of life may yet arise from the corpse of France; that of Germany will be a center of pestilence for all Europe. A nation that has lost its ideals is doomed, and those who breathe its fetid emanations contract the same mortal disease.

"Poor Germany! The cup of the Almighty's anger is poured upon thee as well as upon us; and while thou art rejoicing and growing intoxicated, the philosophic mind is weeping over thy situation and preparing thy epitaph.

"France still holds in her shriveled hands a shred of the starry coat of the future, whilst thou enfoldest thyself in the sullied flag which will serve for thy winding-sheet."

Many of George's last political ideas culminate as of old in a plea for liberty and equality: "The state can force no one to do good. The state is not a better or a wiser person; it is a contract established to safeguard individual rights, and it must not be permitted that, under the pretext of duty, the privileges of one person surpass those of another."

George concluded that free and non-clerical education must be given to every individual. Equality implied that every man should be given time and opportunity to develop his faculties and values, provided they were values and not an inertia. It therefore necessitated the abolishment of over-long working-hours and implied the continual struggle against poverty and misery.

"If it is not liberty and equality for all, let us not try to solve the problem of equality; we are not worthy to define it; we are not able to understand it. Equality cannot be imposed. . . . It cannot grow on the barricades. We have learned this much. The victorious faction will immediately crush it.

"But let equality become a part of our morality. Let it enter into our ideas. Let it have our great patriotic charity —our love. It is senseless to believe that we emerge from a battle still filled with a respect for human rights. All civil war engenders crime."

George could give no solution for the present social problems except this one that involved a slow but definite fusion of individualistic and socialistic impulses within society. But the time was not ripe for it. There was, however, a basic truth from which all social phenomena had to be viewed: "We have not an individual but a collective soul and a collective sense of responsibility, whence springs our great need for human solidarity."

This was the lesson her political life had taught her. But it was now the task of another and younger generation to take this weight of wisdom off her hands.

CHAPTER SEVEN

The Good Lady of Nohant

GEORGE had grown old and she was fast becoming a legend. Lélia had attained the last of her many stages —she was the "good lady of Nohant" now. Calm, peace, and happiness had come to her in the winter of her life. She was in Nohant, watched the things growing in her garden, played with the grandchildren, Aurore and Gabrielle, sewed dresses for Lina, painted sets for the puppet show, talked botany to Maurice, or gave an occasional thought to a plot which stirred in her mind. In her letters to Flaubert she called herself the happiest and most contented of "old troubadours," and she added: "Of course, it has not always been like this. Once I committed the folly of being young."

There she is in her garden now—as the younger Dumas described her:

"It is noon, the hour when everything becomes sharply defined. Regard that woman who descends the steps of the porch. Her hair is gray under her little straw hat: she is all alone, she walks gently in the sun. She talks to the gardener, she bends down to inhale the fragrance of a flower but she does not break it; she stops, listens . . . to what? She herself could not tell you. To something that is not yet and one day will be. She sits down on her stone bench. She has become motionless, has fused into infinity, has become flower, star, breeze, ocean, soul."

The world still came to see her. Flaubert, Dumas *fils*, Jerome Napoleon, and the Russian Turgenev continued their visits to the last. Even Gautier came, in spite of all the sarcastic comments he had made about her. Always welcome were George's friends from the Odéon or the Gymnase, though on the whole George preferred the men to the women there. She had little faith in actresses, who were often inconsistent and cynical, like Sarah Bernhardt, who could weep on her shoulder and threaten suicide one day and next day embark on a new folly.

Nohant continued to keep its atmosphere of noisy gaiety. The puppet show was still the center of attraction and no guest could avoid it, much as he often wanted to. In addition the family members liked to make victims of their guests, especially of the newcomers, by playing more or less harmless jokes on them. George would then stay in hiding and watch the outcome from behind a door. As her doctor, Pestel, said, she had little gaiety of her own, but was in great need of noise and laughter.

In the evening the guests gathered in the great salon, where in true eighteenth-century style they sat around a large oval table. The women were busy with their embroidery or their drawings, the men played chess and dominoes. The conversation turned around literature, generally the latest book by Flaubert, or the political course of Thiers, now head of the government. The guests were careful in voicing their opinions, for they knew their hostess's point of view.

Late at night George returned to her writing-desk. She wrote no more than an hour or so now, but still produced one or two novels a year which the faithful Buloz published in the *Revue des Deux Mondes*. For her themes she drew on the world of the *vieilles comtesses* who once were a target for her mother's sarcasm. George had more tolerance for the friends of her grandmother now than in her youth and took a certain satisfaction in re-creating them. In return the older generation that once scorned her now read her with much gratification.

But love was still her *leitmotiv*—a love which like Rousseau's went beyond all earthly desires and projected itself into a God-conscious infinity. "Yes, love is the key to the enigma of the universe!" she told her friends in her rare communicative moods. "Always to come forth again, to grow and cling to life, to seek one's opposite for the purpose of assimilation, continuously to accomplish the marvel of commingling and combining, whence springs the miracle of new productions—these are the laws of nature."

Her sympathies went beyond her own species. In a final, all-embracing gesture she gathered nature, the universe, and the cosmic soul into her heart. A last synthesis of religion and philosophy led her to a pantheistic conception of the Deity. God is immanent in the universe and all of the universe is in harmony through God. "I am not dreaming when, standing before a great edifice of rock, I feel that these mighty bones of the earth are mine and that the calmness of my mind shares their apparent death and dramatic immobility. 'The moon consumes the stone,' say the peasants. I maintain, it drinks the cold light of the moon and undergoes a silent disintegration during the night from having been subjected to the destructive action of the sun. I think of the hidden work going on in the molecules and I feel inclined to attribute to them an existence similar to our own. I, too, am a stone which time disintegrates; and the tranquillity of these blocks, whose sole function is to submit to the action of day and night, deeply impresses me, calms me, numbs my vitality."

Do we really ever get old? George sometimes asked herself. She was much astonished to find her intellectual capacities as alert as ever. Nothing seemed to stagnate within her.

But to summarize her life or her personality seemed impossible. "Do we ever become a definite person? I do not know. It seems to me that we change from day to day, and that by the end of the year we have turned into a new person."

In the end she summarized nevertheless: "I try in vain to find that former ego of mine which was forever restless, worried, and at odds with itself and the world. I am sure I suffered from megalomania. It was the style of the day; everybody wanted to be great, and because one was not really great, one became desperate. I had to make tremendous efforts to remain good and sincere."

In May 1876 she suffered one of her gastro-enteric attacks which usually sent her to bed for several days. But this time the illness was more persistent. Her condition grew worse and the doctor realized that the disease had entered upon an acute stage which probably would be fatal.

George suffered mentally as well as physically, since the nature of her illness seemed particularly loathsome to her. Neither Maurice nor the grandchildren were allowed to spend much time by her side. Their memory of her must not become distorted by these last days of suffering and disease.

She spoke little; her gaze was absent, as if she were far away, re-treading the tangled paths of her former life.

What had worried her once and roused her passions seemed small and of no importance now: her childish tears for her absent mother; the image of her father; Julie the chambermaid, who had so cruelly beaten her; Grandmother with her blond wig; Casimir's fury; the ecstasy of her first-won freedom; the suffering for Musset's sake; Michel's treason; her great political and socialistic ambitions. Did she really write *Indiana* and *Consuelo?* She did not remember a single word.

Chopin? The blue sound? Did the memory hurt? Had not her inner voices failed when she let him go?

While she lay dying, spring had come to Berry. The countryside was gay with flowers and radiant under a clear sky. Along with friends and relatives who came to visit George, the sweet smell of warm earth and blossoming trees slipped into her darkened room. At night the June moon stood round and bright over the trees in the park.

The moon consumes the stone. George, too, was like the stone, now silently enduring the change of day and night.

Outside in the valley the boatmen signaled to one another as they pulled their barges upstream. The grain grew fast in these early June days. The meadows would soon be ready for their first mowing.

"Let the green . . ." she whispered one evening. Lina and Solange, who were near her, did not catch her meaning. Then they realized that George had uttered a last wish. She wanted the green lawn over her grave. No heavy stone should cover her.

The night before her death she was roused from her apathy. There was a last gesture of rebellion.

"Oh, God, death!" she cried out in terror. She had welcomed him so often, had called him "gentle friend." Did she see him now—as did Turgenev in his last hour—as the horrible shadow against her wall? She passed away on the morning of June 8, 1876, after an agony of four hours. She was seventy-two years old.

The members of her household gathered around her bed. Side by side with Maurice, his wife, and the children, knelt Solange, to whom her mother's illness had finally opened the doors of a home which had been closed to her for many years. In the confusion that followed she took charge of the household, ordered and commanded. Maurice was lost in grief and Lina too tactful to interfere.

Solange, who had become a Catholic some years before, immediately arranged for a Catholic funeral. Revolt and consternation among George's liberal friends! Maurice was torn by doubt and sorrow and could not make up his mind. Should the Church be allowed the last word at the grave of her mother, who had always fought against clerical abuse? Had not his mother explicitly declared herself time and again against a Church funeral?

But George had never officially left the Church, nor were there any special instructions in her will. And Solange insisted: "My mother must not be buried like a dog." The sentence acted like a magic formula on Maurice, and he agreed.

The service took place in the small church of Nohant. The casket set up in the center was adorned with a wreath from the family and a huge wreath from a working-men's association in Paris. Afterwards the peasants carried the coffin to the small cemetery which adjoined George's estate.

The priest spoke a short prayer at the open grave and left immediately after. Paul Meurice, George's collaborator, read a funeral message which Victor Hugo had sent from Guernsey. Flaubert was touched to tears by the long-winded phrases, but Dumas *fils* and Prince Jerome consid-

ered it a piece of declamatory bombast, kept on file for similar occasions by the Grandmaster of literature. Neither
Dumas nor Jerome felt inclined to make a speech after the
clergy and Victor Hugo had had their say.

The sky was dark with clouds. The peasants knelt in the
wet grass, praying. The mourners hurried to shelter from
the driving rain.

Epilogue

THE present is still indebted to George Sand. We do not read her much these days, but we read about her. Every decade produces biographers—and in many countries—who try to throw new light on her personality, her life, and her ideas. Somehow the material seems always different and always in need of new interpretation, though George Sand's philosophic point of view is definitely established as that of the eighteenth century rather than the nineteenth. She belongs to the century of Rousseau, Robespierre, and Babeuf.

The Romantics of 1830—of whom George Sand was one great representative—were the logical commentators of the great liberalistic explosion which we call the French Revolution. They were the torch-bearers of a doctrine demanding full liberty—personal and universal. But as they became aware of the anarchy and confusion which followed the all-too-optimistic economic expansion of the early nineteenth century, they also discovered the needs of the masses. They developed a social conscience, and George Sand, being a preacher and missionary in her work, only lived up to current expectations; if she differed from her writing colleagues at all, it was in intensity and perseverance rather than in subject matter.

Because she touched the popular chords of the time her literary success was great. At one time people spoke of the "century of George Sand," but we today might rather say that she personified its more irrational and popular aspects. She knew her role well and had no illusions as to her abilities. She told Flaubert: "You can write for the future, but I am afraid I shall be forgotten in fifty years. This is the fate of things which are not strictly first class. My idea has rather been to influence some of my contemporaries and to make them share my ideal of sweetness and poetry."

She influenced the world. Victor Hugo called her "the great woman," Renan "the Aeolian harp of all time"; Heine said that "her writings put the world on fire, brightening prisons where no consolation ever entered."

In Germany *Lélia* became a favorite novel-pattern; Poland hailed her as the champion of political freedom; but it was in Russia that she found the greatest admiration and glory. Her social propaganda, so neatly wrapped in the flowery pinafore of romantic plot and phraseology, was never recognized by the watchful Czarist censor and penetrated unimpaired into the farthest corner of holy Russia. Annenkov, Herzen, and Botkin saluted her as an apostle and missionary of the future; the great critic Belinsky called her the greatest poetic glory of the day. More emphatic in their praise were even greater men: Dostoievski, who spoke of the new hope the world gained through her writings, and Turgenev, who explicitly avowed his indebtedness to her teachings.

On the other hand England of the Victorian age was less inclined to give her public applause, though George Sand's outstanding English biographer, Mrs. Schermerhorn, points out that it was less the public than the press that opposed her. The English Puritan of 1840 was vindictive and had, according to William Bolitho, "embarked on one of those terrible drives towards asceticism analogous no doubt to the frenzy for self-mutilation that seizes orgiastic dancers at the extreme height of their passion." The theme of sex-emancipation in Madame Sand's novels probably enraged this Puritan considerably. It was an Italian, Mazzini, then a refugee in England, who in the middle 40's made possible a first English edition of her works. Speaking in her defense, he told the English public that smoking was not immoral, and that it was indelicate to peek into a woman's private life.

Matthew Arnold discovered her as early as 1841, when he came as a student to Oxford, where her books probably were food for the intellectuals. Arnold was so impressed that five years later, after he had graduated and received a fellowship, he set out to visit Nohant. He got there after some difficulty and his note asking for an interview was graciously answered by an invitation to lunch. It was all very thrilling to the young student: the servants in their Berry costume, the red and white Venetian chandelier with its fifty candles, the tablecloth belonging to the Maréchal de Saxe, the cut crystal of Madame Sand, and finally the hostess herself, who welcomed him in the presence of her children and the beautiful-eyed Chopin. "She is all simplicity, frank, cordial simplicity," he wrote after this visit. The charm and spell of those magic hours at Nohant, the memory of George Sand's profoundly generous and benevolent nature, remained with him all his life.

The Brontë sisters and George Eliot, though they took up her battle-cry against the conventionalism and self-righteousness of society, showed no sign in their works that the great French author influenced or even charmed them to any considerable degree. Charlotte Brontë wrote to a friend about 1850 that "fantastic, fanatical, impractical enthusiast as she often is—far from truthful as are many of her views on life—misled as she is apt to be by her feelings

—George Sand has a better nature than Monsieur de Balzac; her brain is larger, her heart warmer than his. *The
Letters of a Traveler* are full of the writer's self, and I never
felt so strongly as in the perusal of this work, that most of
her very faults spring from the excess of her good qualities!" Berating Balzac for his literary realism which made
him show the defects of people rather than their better possibilities, she emphasized once more: "Truly, I like George
Sand better." But Charlotte Brontë did not catch the spark
that lighted the fiery revolt of women in France, Germany,
and Russia. Hers and her sisters' interests were uniquely
turned toward an intellectual and economic liberation of
women, while the demands of the Continental muses went
more toward what the sober Anglo-Saxon mind probably
called libertinism of the heart.

America was similarly shy of the great writer, whose
novels first appeared there in yellow, paper-bound French
editions. They sold cheaply, which made them unpopular
with the American publishers, and they aroused the ire of
the Puritans, who saw a sin in novel-reading anyway. How-
ard Mumford Jones has collected numerous early comments
on George Sand in an article in *American Literature*, January 1932, which make picturesque and amusing reading,
in so far as uncritical personal abuse and strident denunciation can be amusing. The *Southern Literary Messenger* was
one of the more lenient voices in this concert: "George Sand
is possibly worse in her morals than Paul de Kock, but as she
is a lady, or at least a female, we will pass both her and her
novels in expressive silence." A generous soul in the *American Whig Review* of 1845 admitted that at least he preferred her to Lady Byron.

Only a very few of the public utterances were in her
favor, among them those of Margaret Fuller, who in the

Dial gave an account of a visit to Nohant. In describing the personal impression she gained from her first interview with the great French woman, she spoke of the "expression of goodness, nobleness, and power that pervaded the whole . . . the truly human spirit that shone in her heart." She went on to say that "of course there might have been something of the Bacchante in her life, and of the love of night and storm and the free raptures amid which roamed on the mountain-tops the followers of Cybele, the great goddess and mother. But she was never coarse, never gross!"

Since Margaret Fuller, however, was a rebel herself, she may have been partial to this *âme sœur*. But it is sure that she introduced George Sand's work to Emerson and his friends. Charles Cestre in *Harvard et la France* politely indicates that toward the middle of his life the great sage of Concord "had sufficiently freed himself of the fetters of Puritan morals to break the interdict cast on the novel." Emerson began to like Balzac, Dumas *père*, and George Sand. He showed a special liking for the latter and read her books promptly after their publication. He called her a great genius, "one who yet owes to her birth in France her entire freedom from the cant and snuffle of our dead Christianity." *Lucrezia Floriani*, *Jeanne*, *Consuelo*, and *The Sin of Monsieur Antoine* he numbered among the books which give culture to a person. "George Sand," he added naïvely, "is quite conversant with all the ideas that occupy us here in America!" That he should especially have recommended *The Sin of Monsieur Antoine*, the novel which frightened even its author by its daring radicalism, may be explained by what Monsieur Cestre calls "the intimate relationship between the mystic of piety and the mystic of passion."

Comments on George Sand may also be found in the papers of Lowell, Hawthorne, and Longfellow, but they

were short and for private use only. In view of the public's
attitude this restraint is understandable, just as Whitman's
silence on his indebtedness to George Sand may be considered simply as due to caution. Mrs. Shephard, who in a recent Whitman biography traced his ideas and even his costume to the inspiration given by characters in *The Countess
of Rudolstadt*, wonders about his lack of frankness, but his
prestige as poet might have definitely suffered—even in the
50's—had he openly admitted his poetical dependence on
such a questionable source. A gallant and sympathetic defense of George Sand came considerably later and from
such a cool and critical mind as Henry James. In the *North
American Review* are several of his articles on George Sand
published between 1898 and 1912. They show an affection-
ate and fair understanding of a writer whose fame was then
no longer at its height. He calls her "one of the great voices
of that mid-century concert against the last fine strains of
which we are more and more banging the door." He also
feels, like Matthew Arnold and others, that she belonged in
Goethe's family, but that she might have to content herself
there with a silver rather than a gold cup. "She wrote a
hundred books, but no *Faust;* she was to have all the distinction but not all the perfection!"

He scoffs at Balzac for calling her a man and insists that
her abiding value will probably be "in her having given
her sex for its new evolution and transformation, the real
standard and measure of change."

However, her value lies deeper than this. Like Goethe,
Napoleon, Don Juan, Alexander, Cagliostro, and others, she
is one of the great human enigmas which each generation
interprets anew because—in themselves complete—they allow for the development of infinite human aspects. That explains the varied and often contradictory comment on them.

It is hard to synthesize personalities like George Sand's. She may be likened to a crystal, more important by its facets than its size.

What gives her significance for us and raises her from the literary dead is her social attitude: her knowledge of the interrelationship of human beings, her sensing that humanity is but a vast collective soul whose parts cannot be impaired without impairing the whole. Much of her "socialism" is based on the Utopian schemes of her time— schemes which at first seem dated and without immediate value. Their potential value nevertheless remains.

Yes, we are indebted to George Sand. She was great and kind, and admirably transmitted that most vital impulse of the French nation, aiming always to raise the level of justice, understanding, and human dignity.

ACKNOWLEDGMENTS

INDEX

Acknowledgments

The documentary material in this book is taken from George Sand's own writings as well as from many French, English, and German sources.

I am particularly indebted to George Sand's main biographers: Caro, Doumic, Rocheblave, Spoelberch de Lovenjoul, and Karénine. The last has been called the quarry from which the majority took their building material, and I suppose that this is very true.

Concerning Chopin I consulted Ganche and Pourtalès; on Leroux I quoted his excellent biographer Thomas. General historical information was supplied by the works of Thureau-Dangin, Lucas-Dubreton, Thiers, Thierry, Louis Blanc, Gorce, Guedalla, Simpson, and Adam.

With great pleasure I express my gratitude to George Sand's last surviving grandchild, Madame Aurore Lauth-Sand, who gave me several interviews at her Paris home and extended much advice and generous help. The contact with her conveyed an image of her grandmother which was much more intimate and alive than any documentary evidence could be. This is due mainly to a general physical and spiritual resemblance which seems to link the earlier to the later generations in the Sand family. Talking to Madame Lauth-Sand was for that reason almost like talking to George Sand herself.

Finally, my heartfelt thanks must go to Thomas and Jane Culver Polsky for their aid in preparing the manuscript for publication.

F. S.

Index

Agoult, Countess Marie d', 90, 113, 119–20, 123, 127, 130–9, 141, 142, 195
Albert, Minister, 188
Alexander, 274
American Literature, 272
American Whig Review, 272
André (Sand), 88, 89
Annenkov, 270
Antony (Dumas), 51, 216
Arago, Etienne, 195
Aristotle, 29
Arnim, Bettina von, 102, 175
Arnold, Matthew, 271, 274
Arnould-Plessy, Madame, 218
Augustus the Strong, 13, 36
Austen, Jane, 271
Autre, L' (Sand), 251
Avenir, L' (Sand), 124

Babeuf, 107, 114
Ballanche, 121
Balzac, 59–60, 94, 147, 154, 215, 220, 245, 272–4
Barbès, 195, 205, 209
Bazard, 105
Beaumont, Abbé de, 24, 25
Beauvau, Princess de, 141
Belgiojoso, Princess, 132
Belinsky, 270
Benedict, 65, 66
Béranger, 161, 163, 207
Béranger, Madame, 218
Berlioz, 140
Bernardin, 55
Bernhardt, Sarah, 251, 262
Berry, Duc de, 48
Berthelot, 245
Beyle, Henri. *See* Stendhal
Bismarck, 252, 253

Blanc, Louis, 70, 103, 162, 174, 180, 187, 188, 189, 192–3, 194, 199, 209, 256
Blanqui, 195, 256
Bocage, 134, 218
Bolitho, William, 20, 270
Bonaparte, Napoleon, 26, 274
Bonde, Baroness, 200
Botkin, 270
Boucoiran, 44, 78, 79, 91
Bourges, Michel de. *See* Michel de Bourges
Brault, Augustine, 176, 182
Brentano, 63
Briand, 198
Brontë, 271–2
Brotherhoods, 170
Browning, Elizabeth Barrett, 219
Buloz, 66, 69, 72, 78, 82, 89, 91, 93, 110, 147, 151, 163, 243, 263
Buonarroti, 107, 108, 114
Byron, 30, 80, 249
Byron, Lady, 272

Cabet, 195
Cadio (Sand), 250
Cagliostro, 274
Calamatta, Lina. *See* Sand, Lina
Calamatta, Luigi, 154, 226, 231
Capo de Feuillide, 73
Caricature, La, 48
Carlier, 209
Carnot, 189
Caro, 155
Carrel, Armand, 108, 161
Carteret, 195
Caussidière, 188
Cavaignac, 200
Cazamajou, Caroline (*née* Delaborde), 20, 23, 118, 176

281

ne life
ge Sand.

8 1981

8 '82

11,

5

2 0 1980